Guidelines

Questions and Answers about the laws of MUKTZEH

Guidelines

Questions and Answers about the laws of MUKTZEH

Rabbi Elozor Barclay
Rabbi Yitzchok Jaeger

MENUCHA
PUBLISHERS

A Menucha Press Book

First published January 2018
Copyright © 2018 by E. Barclay & Y. Jaeger
ISBN 978-1-61465-487-2

All rights reserved

No part of this publication may be translated, reproduced, stored in a retrieval system, or transmitted in any form or by any means, electronic, mechanical, photocopying, recording, or otherwise, without prior permission in writing from the copyright holders and the publisher.

Please address any questions or comments
regarding the GUIDELINES books to the authors:
E. Barclay (02) 583 0914
Y. Jaeger (02) 583 4889
email: 5834889@gmail.com

VOLUMES IN THE GUIDELINES SERIES:

KIDDUSH & HAVDALAH	HONORING PARENTS
THE THREE WEEKS	YOMIM NORAIM
FAMILY PURITY	CHANUKAH
CHOL HAMOED	BRACHOS
SHEMITTAH	SUCCOS
SHAATNEZ	PURIM
TEFILLAH	YICHUD
YOM TOV	BORER
PESACH	BISHUL

MAJOR EVENTS OF LIFE
MUKTZEH
THE GUIDELINES HAGGADAH
SEFIRAS HA'OMER & SHAVUOS
CANDLE LIGHTING & SEPARATING CHALLAH

Published by:
Menucha Publishers Inc.
250 44th street Suite #B2
Brooklyn N.Y. 11232
Tel/Fax: 718-232-0856
1-855-Menucha
sales@menuchapublishers.com
www.menuchapublishers.com

(Translation of Hebrew Original)

Rabbi CHAIM P. SCHEINBERG
Rosh Hayeshiva "TORAH ORE"
and Morah Hora'ah of Kiryat Mattersdorf

בס"ד, חודש שבט, תשס"ג

מכתב ברכה

I was pleased to see **"Guidelines"**, an impressive six volume work which encompasses the *halachos* of the *Moadim* and other relevant topics, written by Rabbi Elozor Barclay, *shlita* and Rabbi Yitzchok Jaeger, *shlita*. These books have been praised highly by numerous *Gedolei HaRabbonim* and have been received warmly by the English speaking Torah community.

As a matter of policy, I do not endorse *halachic* rulings in any published *sefer*. However, since so many *Gedolei Torah* have already agreed to what is written and offered their approbation to **"Guidelines"**, I join them and offer my heartfelt blessing that *Hashem* should guide and assist the authors in producing more successful *halachic* works, which glorify and strengthen the Torah.

Signed in the honor of the Torah,

Chaim P. Scheinberg

Rabbi Chaim Pinchas Scheinberg

2 Panim Meirot St., Jerusalem, P.O.B. 6979, Tel. (02) 537-1513, Israel

Letter of Approbation received from
Rabbi Nachman Bulman zt"l for Guidelines to Succos

Rabbi Nachman Bulman
Yeshivat Ohr Somayach
Beit Knesset Nachliel

רב נחמן בולמן
מנהל רוחני ישיבת אור שמח
רב ק"ק נחליאל נוה יעקב מזרח

בע"ה

יום ו', י"ח תמוז, תשס"ב פה עיה"ק ת"ו

Friday, eighteenth of Tammuz, 5762, the holy city of Yerushalayim.

I was delighted to see the fifth volume of the **Guidelines** series. The questions and answers in **Guidelines** provide a clear and easily understood format and clarify relevant halachic issues.

It is clear from the quality of this work that Rabbi Elozor Barclay and Rabbi Yitzchok Jaeger have invested great amounts of time and effort in their thorough investigation of these dinim. Every answer has been written carefully and thoughtfully, considering both the classic and the most up-to-date halachic authorities. The accurate Hebrew references will certainly be an invaluable aid for any reader who wishes to investigate further.

I highly recommend this book to any person who is truly searching to know the correct conduct.

Signed with admiration,

נחמן בולמן

מנהל רוחני ישיבת אור שמח
רב ק"ק נחליאל נוה יעקב מזרח ביום הנ"ל
ועיני נשואות לשמים להסכמת שוכן במרומים

משה הלברשטאם

חבר הבד"צ העדה החרדית
ראש ישיבת "דברי חיים" טשאקאווע
מח"ס שו"ת "דברי משה"
פעיה"ק ירושלים תובב"א
רח' יואל 8 טל. 5370514

בס"ד

ערב ט"ו בשבט לסדר "והיה ביום הששי" תשס"ג לפ"ק

מאד שמחתי ונהנתי כשהובאו לפני ליקוטים נפלאים לעת עתה על הלכות פורים, פסח, ימים נוראים, סוכה וחנוכה ואי"ה עוד יד נטוי' להשלים המלאכה, שחיברו האברכים החשובים חו"ב מוהר"ר אלעזר ברקלי שליט"א ומוהר"ר יצחק ייגר שליט"א אוצר בלום מה שאספו וליקטו הלכות רבות ונחוצות מהשו"ע ונושאי כליו מספרי הפוסקים ראשונים ואחרונים מסודר בתבונה והשכל בטטו"ד לתועלת וזיכוי הרבים.

ונוכחתי לראות כי הלכו מישרים לאסוקי שמעתתא אליבא דהלכתא והיטב אשר עשו שציינו מקור לכל הלכה והלכה למען אשר כבר הזהירו גאוני קדמאי שלא לפסוק הלכה למעשה מספרי הקיצורים.

ואמינא לפעלא טבא יישר כוחם וחילם לאורייתא והנני נותן להם בזה ברכת מו"ר הגה"צ שליט"א שיזכו להמשיך לעלות במעלות התורה להו"ל עוד חיבורים יקרים ולזכות את הרבים מתוך נחת ושפע ברכות והצלחה, אכי"ר.

ובעה"ח בפקודת הקודש
יהונתן וינר
מו"צ בבית הוראה
שע"י מרן הגה"צ שליט"א

נ.ב. בספר על הלכות חנוכה שאלה 15, בגדר איסור מלאכה לנשים בחנוכה עיין בן איש חי פרשת וישב סי' כז, וט"ז ס' תרע סק"ב דמשמע דומיא דר"ח, וכן שמעתי מכרכא דכולי ביה מרא דכולא תלמודא (לשון מוהר"ר הגה"צ בשו"ת דברי משה ס' יד) ממוהר"ר חיים קנייבסקי שליט"א.

*Letter of Approbation received from
Rabbi Pesach Eliyahu Falk for Guidelines to Tefillah*

Rabbi E. Falk

146 Whitehall Road
Gateshead NE8 1TP
England

פסח אליהו פאלק

דומ"ץ בקה"ק גייטסהעד יצ"ו
מח"ס שו"ת מחזה אליהו
יזכור ושמור' על הלכות שבת
'עוז והדר לבושה' על הל' צניעות דלבוש

בס"ד

20 Kisleiv 5765 - Gateshead UK

Once again a great service has been rendered to the Jewish English-speaking public by the great "partners in *zikuy harabim*" - Rabbi Elozor Barclay *shlita* and Rabbi Yitzchok Jaeger *shlita*. They have prepared a sefer on the laws of *tefilla* - thereby giving the person who is praying easy access to the numerous intricate laws that could apply to him at any point during his prayers. With this production they have earned themselves an enormous merit, for *tefilla* is a duty that stands towering above everything else (See *Gemara Brachos* 32b), and to ensure the correct execution of such a duty by a multitude of people, is an immeasurable merit.

As with their other works in the **"Guidelines"** series, this *sefer* is concise, accurate, and well structured. The authors have performed a great service, presenting these vital and complex laws in a clear and straightforward questions and answers format. This style arouses the interest and opens the mind, enabling the reader to fully integrate the information. As clarity of material assists the memory, the person who learns the relevant *halachos* in this manner is likely to remember them and know exactly how to react when a given situation arises.

Unfortunately, my busy schedule does not allow me to thoroughly review every *halacha*, and therefore I cannot accept personal responsibility for the rulings given. However, the authors have themselves invested vast amounts of time and effort researching the sources and clarifying the laws. Apart from this, they have had access to the excellent *seforim* that have been published on the laws of *tefilla* over the last two decades. I am therefore confident that the *halachos* have been correctly presented and I add my approval to its printing for the benefit of the public.

May *Hashem Yisborach* bless the authors with great success in the publication of this work, and other works that they will produce *b'ezer Hashem* in the future. I pray that this *sefer* will be warmly accepted and will lead to increased appreciation and greater dedication to the great gift *Hashem Yisborach* has given us - the means to approach Him thrice daily and present our needs to Him through the medium of *tefilla*.

With Torah blessings,

Rabbi Pesach Eliyahu Falk

הרב רפאל צבי ובר
רב דקהילת קמניץ
ונוה יעקב מזרח, ירושלים

ז' כסלו תשס"ד
בס"ד

מכתב ברכה

שמחתי לראות ששני תלמידי חכמים יקרים הרב אלעזר ברקלי שליט"א והרב יצחק ייגר שליט"א חיברו ספר פסקי הלכות בשפה האנגלית.

וכבר זכו לחבר פסקי הלכות על המועדים שהתפרסמו הרבה, וזיכו את הרבים. ויש תועלת רבה בצורת הכתיבה בלשון שאלות ותשובות ועי"ז מתבררת ההלכה היטב.

ואע"פ שאיני מבין שפה האנגלית, אבל אני מכירם ויודעם בהשתדלות לאסוקי שמעתתא אליבא דהלכתא, ונשאו ונתנו אתי בהרבה נושאים, והנני מברכם שיקבלו דבריהם בביהמ"ד.

בברכת התורה,

צבי ובר

RABBI ZEV LEFF
Rabbi of Moshav Matisyahu
Rosh Hayeshiva Yeshiva Gedola Matisyahu

בס"ד
תמוז תשס"ז

It is with great pleasure that I have received the latest addition to the series of Halachic Guides produced by Rabbi Elozor Barclay שליט"א and Rabbi Yitzchok Jaeger שליט"א - **Guidelines** to Shemittah.

This is an impressive work which will serve as an invaluable aid to those who seek to be guided through the shemittah year.

As in the previous volumes the laws are lucidly and concisely presented in a manner that will serve as a guide and source for the beginner and a source of review for the advanced student. I highly recommend this work as all the other volumes of this series.

May Hashem grant the authors long life and health and ability to continue to merit Klal Yisroel with the promulgation of Torah and mitzvos.

With Torah blessings,

Rabbi Zev Leff

Table of Contents

Foreword **15**

Chapter One: General Principles **17**

Chapter Two: Non-muktzeh Items **22**

Chapter Three: Kli Shemelachto L'issur **28**

Chapter Four: Electrical Appliances **40**

Chapter Five: Muktzeh Machmas Chisaron Kis **47**

Chapter Six: Muktzeh Machmas Gufo **55**

Chapter Seven: Designation **77**

Chapter Eight: Muktzeh Machmas Issur **82**

Chapter Nine: Muktzeh Machmas Mitzvah **101**

Chapter Ten: Nolad **106**

Chapter Eleven: Bosis **110**

Chapter Twelve: Pockets and Drawers **130**

Chapter Thirteen: Different Types of Movement **136**

Chapter Fourteen: Fixed Status **143**

Chapter Fifteen: Nullifying a Item's Usage **149**

Chapter Sixteen: Exceptional Circumstances **155**

Chapter Seventeen: Yom Tov **163**

Glossary **168**

Index **171**

Hebrew Sources **183**

Foreword

With praise and thanks to Hashem, we continue the Guidelines series on the laws of Shabbos with the present volume on the laws of muktzeh.

One of the great challenges of this subject is categorizing the huge variety of articles found around the house. In the days of old, there were probably at most a few hundred objects in a typical home. Today, it is no exaggeration to say that one can find in an average home many thousands of items. Knowing whether one may or may not move any particular article therefore requires much study and careful analysis. We highly recommend the useful reference book called "The Muktzeh Directory" by Rabbi Y Ben Tzur, *shlita*, which lists over three thousand items.

Of all the laws of Shabbos, those of muktzeh are among the most applicable since one's hands are in constant use, and moving articles from place to place is almost second nature and is done without a moment's thought. Rabbi Yonasan Walliner zt"l, wrote a list of instructions for God-fearing people entitled "*Marganisa Tova*", a precious jewel. (It is sometimes printed at the end of the Chofetz Chaim's *sefer*, *Ahavas Chesed*.) In point number thirty he writes: "Do not move your hands on Shabbos and Yom Tov to do anything unless you first pay attention and investigate whether this does not involve a desecration of Shabbos or Yom Tov, *chas veshalom*." This warning is certainly appropriate in regard to the restrictions of muktzeh.

Using the Guidelines Question and Answer style, we have attempted to present the laws in a clear and systematic manner and have provided numerous examples that demonstrate the application of each concept.

Rarely will a written work be a perfect substitute for a one-to-one discussion with a Rav. The answer to a query often depends upon various factors that only further questioning can clarify. Even though much thought and effort has been invested in the phrasing and wording used, it is possible that *halachos* may be misunderstood or misconstrued. Our primary intent is to guide the reader through these laws, hence the title Guidelines.

We would like to express our thanks to Rav Yaakov Montrose *shlita*, author of the Halachic World series, who with his keen perception and comprehensive mastery of the topics provided many valuable changes and additions throughout the entire book. Many thanks also to Reb Yerachmiel Goldberg, Reb Yerachmiel Stander, and Reb Pinchas Goldstein for meticulously checking the text.

It is our hope that in the merit of fulfilling the laws of Shabbos punctiliously, we will be worthy to experience the peace, prosperity, and blessings that are promised to those who guard the Shabbos.

Elozor Barclay　　　　　　　　　　　　Yitzchok Jaeger

Teves 5778

Chapter One
General Principles

1. What is muktzeh?

Literally it means 'set apart'. However, the term is used to describe an item that may not be moved on Shabbos. The opposite of muktzeh is *muchan*, meaning 'prepared'. In a very general sense, one could say that objects which are ready for use on Shabbos are not muktzeh, whereas objects that are not ready for use are muktzeh. See also Question 11.

2. Is this a Torah prohibition?

There is an allusion to the concept of muktzeh in the verse, "And it will be on the sixth day, and they shall prepare what they will bring" (*Shemos* 16:5). Nevertheless, the laws of muktzeh were instituted by *Chazal* during the early years of the second *Beis Hamikdash*. At that time, Shabbos observance was unfortunately very neglected, and many people were even desecrating the holy day in public. The restrictions of muktzeh were introduced in order to prevent forbidden activities and to enhance the *kedusha* of Shabbos.

Note: The Rabbinic prohibitions of Shabbos are almost like Torah law since they are based on the Torah principle that Shabbos should be a day of rest.

3. How do the laws of muktzeh protect Shabbos?

The following explanations have been given:

- The *navi Yeshayahu* several generations earlier had already warned that one must not walk or talk on Shabbos as one does on a weekday (*Yeshayahu* 58:13). By extension, *Chazal* added the restriction not to handle all items freely. If one were allowed to move any object that he wishes, he might spend time organizing household tools or clearing stones in the garden, and Shabbos would cease to be a day of rest.

- Many items of muktzeh are utensils used to do a *melacha* that is forbidden on Shabbos. Since one may not handle such an object, he will not come to do a *melacha* with it. For example, if one would be allowed to move a pen, he might forget and write with it.

- Some people are not engaged in work even during the week, and Shabbos for them is not very different from a weekday. The restriction of muktzeh adds another aspect of rest for such people.

- If a person would be allowed to move objects without restriction, he might accidentally take something from the house to the street. The laws of muktzeh are thus a safeguard against the specific *melacha* of carrying.

4. May one touch a muktzeh object?

Yes, provided that it does not move even slightly. For example, one may touch a washing machine, but one may not touch the leaf of a tree since it will inevitably move slightly. See Question 148.

5. May one use a muktzeh object?

Yes, provided that it does not move even slightly. For example, one may place an item on top of a microwave.

6. May a muktzeh object be moved in a different way?

This is permitted under certain conditions. See Chapter Thirteen for details.

7. Do all muktzeh items have the same laws?

No, there are four basic categories of muktzeh with variant laws. They are:

1. *Kli shemelachto l'issur* – an item used primarily for something forbidden on Shabbos. For example, a hammer. See Chapter Three.

2. *Muktzeh machmas chisaron kis* – muktzeh due to potential monetary loss. For example, a *shechita* knife. See Chapter Five.

3. *Muktzeh machmas gufo* – an item that by its nature is not prepared for Shabbos use. For example, garbage. See Chapter Six.

4. *Bosis* – an item used as a base for a muktzeh object. For example, a drawer containing money. See Chapter Eleven.

8. Must non-muktzeh items be prepared before Shabbos?

No, a person is not required to do or even think anything in order to prepare an item for use on Shabbos. Any object that does not fit into one of the above categories is considered to be automatically prepared and is therefore not muktzeh.

9. What are examples of non-muktzeh items?

Among the most common are: edible food, tableware, *sefarim*, clothing, and furniture. See Chapter Two.

10. Can an item change its status during Shabbos?

- An item that was muktzeh at the beginning of Shabbos usually remains muktzeh throughout Shabbos even if the reason for its being muktzeh no longer applies. For example, if money was placed on a table before Shabbos and it was knocked off during Shabbos, the table remains a muktzeh *bosis*. See Chapter Fourteen for more details.
- An item that was not muktzeh at the beginning of Shabbos can become muktzeh on Shabbos. For example, after one has shelled an egg, the shell is muktzeh. See Question 209.

11. What if an item did not exist before Shabbos?

An item that came into existence on Shabbos is called *nolad*, literally meaning 'born'. It is muktzeh since it was not ready for use at the beginning of Shabbos. For example, a newly laid egg. See Chapter Ten for more details.

12. Do the laws of muktzeh apply on Yom Tov?

Basically, yes. However, in many cases the laws are more lenient, and in a few cases they are even more stringent than on Shabbos. When Yom Tov is on Shabbos, the Shabbos rules apply. The Shabbos rules also apply on Yom Kippur even when it is on a weekday. See Chapter Seventeen for details.

13. Do the laws of muktzeh apply on *Chol Hamoed*?

No. All types of muktzeh items may be moved for any reason.

Chapter Two
Non-muktzeh items

14. May non-muktzeh items be moved freely?
Certain non-muktzeh items may be moved without any restriction whatsoever. Others may be moved for any purpose but not when there is absolutely no reason for moving them.

15. Which items may be moved without restriction?
- *Sefarim*. This includes all types of Torah literature and notes.
- Edible foods and drinks.
- Tableware. This includes plates, bowls, cups, and cutlery.
- Clothes.
- Jewelry, including a watch.
- Perfume, snuff, deodorant spray and roll-on.
- Glasses.

16. Could such items ever be muktzeh?
Yes, they could all be muktzeh by becoming a *bosis*. Additionally, with the exception of *sefarim* and food, they could become *muktzeh machmas chisaron kis*.

17. Which non-muktzeh items are restricted?

All non-muktzeh items besides those listed above. Examples include: Air freshener spray, bed linen, blech, dishcloths, egg slicer, furniture, liquid soap, ornaments, keys, secular books (but see Question 58), stroller, tablecloths, many toys (see next section). Such an item is called a *kli shemelachto le'heter*.

18. When may such an item be moved?

It may be moved for any of the following reasons:
- To use it either immediately or later in the day.
- To use the place where it is situated either immediately or later in the day.
- To protect it from loss or damage.
- To tidy the room.

19. When may such an item not be moved?

It may not be moved if there is absolutely no reason to do so, e.g. out of total absentmindedness.

20. What if such movements have a calming effect on the person?

This is an acceptable reason, and such moving is permitted. Similarly, one may move the item in order to enhance one's concentration, e.g. to rock a *shtender* while studying, to play with a "spinner".

21. Is an antique *sefer* muktzeh?

If one reads from it even only occasionally, it is not muktzeh. However, if it is never read but owned only as an investment, it is muktzeh.

22. Is a torn page from a *sefer* muktzeh?

If any part of it is readable, it is not muktzeh; otherwise, it is muktzeh.

23. What if an unreadable page is on the floor?

Opinions differ whether one may pick it up in order to prevent its disgrace. Therefore, it is preferable to move it in an indirect or unusual way (see Chapter Thirteen).

Toys

The subject of toys and games on Shabbos is both broad and complicated. This is because of the enormous variety of toys available today and because their use can involve a wide range of forbidden activities. (The Muktzeh Directory by Rabbi Y. Ben Tzur lists over three hundred entries for toys.) Generally, children over bar/bas mitzvah and certainly adults should try to refrain from playing any type of game on Shabbos, and they should rather occupy themselves with spiritual pursuits. Children below bar/bas mitzvah may play with toys and games that are not muktzeh provided this does not involve any Shabbos prohibition.

24. May very young children play with muktzeh toys?

Children who are too young to understand about Shabbos (approx. below three) may play with muktzeh toys. An adult may not hand a muktzeh toy to the child, but if the child takes it by himself the adult is not required to interfere.

25. Could playing with a non-muktzeh toy involve a prohibition?

Yes. For example:
- Marbles are not muktzeh, but one may not roll them outdoors.
- Some types of building toys are not muktzeh, but one may not use them to construct a model of an object such as a ship or house.
- Toy beads are not muktzeh and may be threaded on a string, but it is forbidden to tie a knot in the string.
- Non-muktzeh games in which one usually writes while playing. These may not be played since this could lead to writing.
- A ball is not muktzeh, but one may not play outdoors where there is no *eiruv*.

Note: These are only a few of the issues involved in toys and games. As explained in the introduction, the topic is complex and cannot be treated fully in this *sefer*. Some more common examples will be mentioned.

26. Are bicycles muktzeh?

- A bicycle is muktzeh since one may not ride it on Shabbos.
- A tricycle is not muktzeh and may be used indoors or outdoors where there is an *eiruv*.

27. Is a jigsaw puzzle muktzeh?

- If the pieces fit together tightly, it is forbidden to connect them and therefore they are muktzeh.
- If the pieces fit together loosely, opinions differ whether one may connect them. Nevertheless, they are not muktzeh.

28. Is a rattle muktzeh?

Opinions differ whether it is muktzeh. In any event, an adult may only move it if he can do so without making it sound.

29. Are musical instruments muktzeh?

Yes, whether they are designed for children or adults.

30. Is a doll muktzeh?

- A regular doll is not muktzeh. (**Note:** If a piece is detached, one may not reattach it if the connection is tight.)
- A doll that makes a noise when squeezed is not muktzeh, but one may not squeeze it.

31. Is a wind-up toy muktzeh?

No. However, an adult should not wind it up but a child may. If the toy emits a noise, it should not be wound up even by a child.

32. Are battery operated toys muktzeh?

Yes. See also Question 456.

33. Are interlocking toys muktzeh?

- If the pieces do not connect tightly, they are not muktzeh.
- If the pieces connect tightly, opinions differ whether they may be used and accordingly differ whether they are muktzeh.

34. Is a balloon muktzeh?

- A balloon that is inflated and tied is not muktzeh.
- A new balloon that has never been inflated is muktzeh since it is forbidden to inflate it on Shabbos for the first time.
- A balloon that has been inflated and deflated may be reinflated only if one usually closes it with a rubber band or stopper. One may not reinflate it if he usually ties it with a knot. Whether it is muktzeh depends on the above possibilities.

The same rules apply to a beach ball or other inflatable shapes.

35. Is play-doh muktzeh?

Yes, since it is forbidden to make shapes with it. The same applies to similar materials, e.g. plasticine.

36. Is a magnet muktzeh?

No.

Chapter Three
Kli Shemelachto L'issur

37. What is a *kli shemelachto l'issur*?

The basic definition is: an article whose normal use is forbidden on Shabbos, whether by the Torah or Rabbinically.

38. Must the article have a secondary use?

• According to some opinions, it must have a secondary use that is permitted on Shabbos in order to be called a *kli shemelachto l'issur*. For convenience, we shall refer to such an item as "type one". Otherwise, it is classified as *muktzeh machmas gufo*.

• According to other opinions, it is a *kli shemelachto l'issur* even if there is no secondary permitted use. We shall refer to such an item as "type two". It is preferable to be stringent and only move type two items in an indirect or unusual way (see Question 60).

39. What are examples of type one?

• A hammer: its primary use is for building; its secondary use is for cracking nuts open.

• A needle: its primary use is for sewing; its secondary use is for removing splinters.

• An empty pot: its primary use is for cooking; its secondary use is for storing food.

Chapter Three - Kli Shemelachto L'issur

40. What are other examples of type one?

Clothes brush, comb, floor squeegee (a counter squeegee is not muktzeh), floor rag, hairbrush*, ironing board, mop, peeler, ruler, scissors, screwdriver, shoe brush, steel wool, toothbrush**, tweezers, umbrella.

*unless it has very soft bristles and is set aside for Shabbos use.

** unless it is a soft brush set aside for Shabbos use. (It may be used only without toothpaste or water.)

41. What are examples of type two?

Battery, bicycle, blow-dryer, calculator, chalk, eraser, flashlight, garden tools, grater, nail file, nails, paintbrush, saw, scale (electronic), screws, sifter, tape measure, toaster, vacuum cleaner.

These items have no permitted secondary use, and therefore opinions differ whether they are considered a *kli shemelachto l'issur*.

42. What if an item has a rarely needed secondary use?

This is still considered a secondary use provided that people actually use it that way occasionally. For example, a screwdriver is sometimes used to open a door whose handle has fallen off, and it is therefore considered a *kli shemelachto l'issur* type one.

43. Which type is a pen?

A pen has secondary uses such as a pointer when teaching a child to read or as a bookmark. Therefore, it is a *kli shemelachto l'issur* type one.

44. Is using an item as a paperweight considered a secondary use?

This qualifies as a secondary use only if a specific item is usually left on a table and is often used as a paperweight.

45. What if a pot is used more often for storing food than cooking?

Since it is designed primarily for cooking, it is a *kli shemelachto l'issur* (type one). The fact that it is used more often for storing food does not justify calling it a non-muktzeh item.

46. Does the same apply to Pyrex dishes?

No. Since Pyrex dishes are designed equally for both cooking and serving food, they are considered as non-muktzeh items. This is true even if they are used more often for cooking.

47. How are empty pans classified?

Pans are clearly designed for frying and baking and are therefore considered *kli shemelachto l'issur* (type one). This also applies to disposable pans.

48. Is a pot or a pan containing food muktzeh?

No. In this case, the pot or the pan is subservient to the food and is not muktzeh.

49. Must there be a minimum quantity of food?

No. However, if almost all the food has been removed and no one is interested in the remnants, the pot becomes muktzeh (*kli shemelachto l'issur*). See also Question 79.

50. What if some food is returned to the pot?

The pot becomes again non-muktzeh.

51. What if the leftovers are placed in a different empty pot?

The second pot remains muktzeh. Only the original pot in which the food was cooked is subservient to the food and is not muktzeh while it contains the food.

52. Is a pot cover muktzeh?

The cover adopts the same laws as the pot with which it is used. Therefore if the pot is empty, the cover is a *kli shemelachto l'issur*, and if the pot contains food, the cover is not muktzeh.

53. Are there other types of *kli shemelachto l'issur*?

Yes. The following types of articles are *kli shemelachto l'issur*:

- An item that is designated for holding muktzeh is a *kli shemelachto l'issur* (type one) when empty. (It is a *bosis* when it is holding muktzeh.) For example: empty *tzedaka* box, purse, or garbage bin.
- An item that assists in doing an activity forbidden on Shabbos. For example: telephone directory (type one), instruction leaflet for an electric appliance (type two).
- An electric or battery appliance that is on but is often switched off, even if it does not do any *melacha* when working. For example: a fan. See Chapter Four.

54. Why is a telephone directory type one?

The primary use of the directory is to find a telephone number, which is forbidden. However, it has secondary permitted uses such as to find an address that is needed on Shabbos, as a booster seat, or as a paperweight. Therefore, it is a *kli shemelachto l'issur* type one.

55. Is a cookbook muktzeh?

Yes. Its primary use is to learn how to cook various foods, and therefore it assists in doing a *melacha*. However, it has a secondary permitted use, namely to learn how to prepare a food that does not require cooking, such as making a salad. Therefore, it is a *kli shemelachto l'issur* type one.

56. Is a sales catalogue muktzeh?

Yes, it is a *kli shemelachto l'issur* since it is forbidden to read it on Shabbos. However, a thick one has a secondary permitted use, namely as a booster seat for a child, and therefore it is a *kli shemelachto l'issur* type one.

57. Is a science book muktzeh?

No, since it is permitted to read any book of secular knowledge on Shabbos. This includes mathematics, medicine, geography, astronomy, biology, etc.
Note: It is praiseworthy to refrain from reading such material on Shabbos and only read matters of Torah.

58. Is a fiction book muktzeh?

- If it is written with the aim of teaching Torah morals, it may be read and is not muktzeh.
- Other fiction books should not be read according to most opinions. According to this view, such books are *kli shemelachto l'issur* type two. According to some opinions, a person may read such books if this provides significant Shabbos enjoyment, and they are not muktzeh.

59. Is a newspaper muktzeh?

This depends on the contents of the newspaper.
- If the entire newspaper is devoted to business news, it is forbidden to read it on Shabbos, and therefore it is muktzeh.
- If the newspaper includes a variety of subjects, such as news, business, Torah topics, health, science,

etc., it is not muktzeh. However, it is forbidden to read the business news and advertisements, and according to most opinions other news. It is therefore strongly recommended not to read any newspaper on Shabbos since it is difficult to avoid reading forbidden sections. The same applies to Torah magazines.

Note: It is advisable not to read a secular newspaper even on a weekday since the views expressed are often contrary to the Torah.

Laws

60. What are the laws of a *kli shemelachto l'issur*?

This category of muktzeh has more lenient laws than categories two and three (see Question 7; regarding a *bosis* see Question 351), and one is sometimes permitted to move such an item. The basic rules of a *kli shemelachto l'issur* are as follows:

1. It may be moved regularly if it is needed for some permitted use.

2. It may be moved regularly if one needs to use the place where it is lying. See Question 68.

3. It may not be moved regularly in order to protect it from loss or damage. See Question 75. However, one may move it with one's body, see Question 440.

61. What is an example of the first rule?

One may use a hammer to crack open nuts.

62. What if one has a nutcracker?

A *kli shemelachto l'issur* may be moved regularly when needed only if he does not have a non-muktzeh item for that need. For example, if he has a nutcracker, he must use that rather than a hammer since a nutcracker is not muktzeh.

63. What if a nutcracker is not easily available?

Opinions differ as to what degree of effort should be expended to avoid using a hammer. For example, the hammer is nearby but the nutcracker is in another room or the hammer is easier to use than the nutcracker. One is certainly not required to borrow a nutcracker from a neighbor rather than use a hammer. Similarly, if a nutcracker is totally unsuitable, one may use a hammer. For example, to crack open a coconut.

64. What if the nutcracker is in use?

If two people wish to crack open nuts at the same time and one is using a nutcracker, the second person may use a hammer. He is not required to wait until the first person has finished using the nutcracker in order to avoid using the hammer.

65. May one pass a *kli shemelachto l'issur* to someone who needs it?

Yes. Passing it is also considered to be using it since he is assisting the person who needs it. However, one may not pass it to a gentile who needs it.

66. May one give a *kli shemelachto l'issur* to a child who wishes to play with it?

Yes, provided that the child is not interested in playing with a non-muktzeh toy.

67. Must the item be used immediately?

No. One may move a *kli shemelachto l'issur* to be available for use later in the day.

68. What is an example of moving it to use its place?

If a hammer was accidentally left on a chair and one wishes to sit there, he may move the hammer.

69. What if another chair is available?

According to most opinions, he may nevertheless remove the hammer if he prefers to sit on that chair.

70. Must the place be used immediately?

No. One may move a *kli shemelachto l'issur* to clear a place that is needed later in the day.

71. What if a *kli shemelachto l'issur* is blocking one's way?

It may be moved since this is considered as needing the place where the article is lying. For example:
- One may move aside an empty pot or pan in a cabinet in order to reach a bowl behind it.
- One may remove *tefillin* that were left on one's tallis in order to wear the tallis.

72. Why are *tefillin* considered a *kli shemelachto l'issur*?

Their primary use is wearing them, which is forbidden on Shabbos. However, they have a secondary use to assist in the study of the laws of *tefillin*. Therefore, they are classified as a *kli shemelachto l'issur* type one.

73. Is it preferable to move a *kli shemelachto l'issur* in an indirect or unusual way?

No. Whenever it is permitted to move a *kli shemelachto l'issur*, i.e. to use it or to clear its place, one may move it in the regular way.

74. Must the item be put down as soon as possible?

No. Since he is permitted to pick it up, he may carry it to any convenient place after he has used it or after he has cleared its place. Nevertheless, he should not continue to hold it for longer than necessary. See also Question 503.

75. What is an example of not moving it to protect it?

If a hammer was left outside and one is concerned that it might be stolen or be ruined by the rain, he may not pick it up and bring it inside. However, he may move it with his body or cover it, see Questions 440 and 441.

76. May one ask a gentile to bring it inside?

Yes. See also Question 446 for other examples when one may ask a gentile to move muktzeh.

77. May one invent a pretext to use it?

One may invent a pretext to use a *kli shemelachto l'issur* in order to protect it from damage or loss. For example, if a hammer was left outside, one may decide to use it to crack open some nuts in the house. However, this is only permitted if there is no nutcracker available to crack open the nuts.

78. May one invent a pretext to use its place?

One may invent a pretext to use the place of a *kli shemelachto l'issur* in order to protect the item from damage or loss. For example, if *tefillin* were left on a chair outside, one may decide to sit on the chair for a while in order to bring the *tefillin* inside.

79. May one remove a *kli shemelachto l'issur* to make the room tidy?

No, this is not considered as using its place. For example, dirty pots and pans may not be removed from the kitchen table or counter to make the room tidy. If necessary, one may move them in an indirect or unusual way. See Question 427. If one is repulsed by the sight of the dirty utensils, he may move them directly (see Question 497). Similarly, one may move them if the space is needed to prepare food, whether immediately or later in the day.

80. May one invent a pretext to use the place in order to make the room tidy?

No, one is only permitted to invent a pretext in order to protect a *kli shemelachto l'issur* from damage or loss. Therefore, the dirty utensils may be moved only if the place is really needed. A simple suggestion to avoid the problem of moving a dirty empty pot is to hold the pot while serving the last portion. Since the pot was not yet muktzeh at that time, one may continue to hold it and move it to a convenient place after it is empty and becomes muktzeh. See Question 503.

Chapter Four
Electric Appliances

81. Is an electric fan muktzeh?
Yes, it is a *kli shemelachto l'issur*. Although it does not do any *melacha* when working, nevertheless it is muktzeh since switching it on is a forbidden activity.

82. Is a fan a *kli shemelachto l'issur* type one or type two?
- When it is switched on, it is type one.
- When it is switched off, it is type two.

83. What if it goes off during Shabbos with a timer and on again later?
It is considered as type one even while it is off.

84. May a person turn a fan towards him for more breeze?
Yes, this is considered as using it.

85. May one turn it away if the breeze is disturbing?
Yes, this is considered as needing its place since it is disturbing one's use of that position.

86. May one adjust the vents of an air-conditioner?

Yes.

87. Is an oven door muktzeh?

Yes. An oven is used primarily for cooking, and therefore the door that assists in its use is classified as a *kli shemelachto l'issur*. However, since the oven is also used for storing empty pans, the door is a *kli shemelachto l'issur* type one. Therefore, one may open the door to take food out since it is blocking the way. Similarly, one may close the door to protect any remaining food or in order to avoid bumping into it.

Note: The door may not be opened or closed if this will cause a light, fan, or heating element to switch on or off.

88. May one open the door to place an empty pot inside the oven?

Yes, if he prefers to store the pot there. The empty pot is also a *kli shemelachto l'issur* and may only be moved according to the rules of such items.

89. Is the door of a dryer muktzeh?

Yes, it is *kli shemelachto l'issur* type one for the same reason as an oven door. Therefore, one may open the door to remove a garment, but one may only close it if he is concerned about bumping into it. See also note in Question 87.

90. Is the door of a dishwasher muktzeh?

Yes, it is a *kli shemelachto l'issur* type one for the same reason as the door of an oven or dryer. Therefore, one may open the door to take out or put in utensils, but one may only close it if he is concerned about bumping into it.

91. Is the door of a washing machine muktzeh?

Yes, it is *kli shemelachto l'issur* type one since dirty clothes are sometimes stored in the machine before they are washed. Therefore, the rules of the previous question apply.

92. Is the door of a car muktzeh?

Yes, it is a *kli shemelachto l'issur* type one since a car is used not only for driving but also to store articles. Therefore, one may open the door to take a needed item from the car provided this will not trigger a light or alarm to go on. The door may be closed again in order to protect non-muktzeh items remaining in the car or if the open door is blocking one's way (e.g. in a narrow garage). The door may not be closed solely to protect the car unless one uses an unusual method (see Question 440). The same applies to the door of the trunk.

Note: One should try to avoid opening the door when other people can see since such an activity looks odd.

Chapter Four - Electrical Appliances

93. Is the door of a refrigerator muktzeh?

No. A refrigerator is comparable to a watch since it is working continually and is not switched on and off regularly (see Question 102). It is possible that the refrigerator is *muktzeh machmas chisaron kis* if it is rarely moved (see Question 120), but this does not apply to the door which is constantly opened and closed. Similarly, the door of a freezer is not muktzeh.

Note: Almost all refrigerators manufactured in the last ten years are electronically programmed to react whenever the door is opened. Such a refrigerator should be adjusted by a competent technician who will connect a Shabbos switch that deactivates the program. One is then permitted to open the door at any time.

94. What if there are muktzeh items in the door?

Many raw foods are muktzeh (category three) since they are inedible. For example: meat, fish, flour, rice (see Question 156). Even if such items are kept in the door of a refrigerator or freezer, the door is not a muktzeh *bosis* (compare Question 399). Nevertheless, it is preferable to store such items inside the refrigerator or freezer rather than in the door.

95. Is a hotplate muktzeh?
- If it is connected, it is a muktzeh *bosis*.
- If it is disconnected, it is a *kli shemelachto l'issur* type one.

96. Is an electric kettle muktzeh?

- An electric kettle or urn that is disconnected is a *kli shemelachto l'issur* type one. Its primary use is to boil water, and its secondary use is to hold boiled water. If it contains water, it is like a pot that contains food and is not muktzeh (see Question 48).

- If the kettle or urn is connected to the electricity and in use, it is a muktzeh *bosis* since the heating element is considered like a flame. Therefore, it may only be moved in an unusual way. Nevertheless, the faucet or pump is not muktzeh and may be used to take out hot water.

97. Is the base of a removable electric kettle muktzeh?

It is a *kli shemelachto l'issur* type two since it has no secondary use.

98. Is a crockpot muktzeh?

- The inner pot has the laws of a regular pot (see Questions 39 and 48).

- The outer pot is a muktzeh *bosis* when connected to the electricity. If it is disconnected, it is a *kli shemelachto l'issur* type two.

99. Is a movable radiator muktzeh?

- If it is connected, it is a muktzeh *bosis* and may only be moved in an unusual way.

- If it is disconnected, it is a *kli shemelachto l'issur* type one since some people place items on it, see Question 42.

Chapter Four - Electrical Appliances

100. Is a table lamp muktzeh?
- If it is switched on, it is a muktzeh *bosis*.
- If it is switched off, it is a *kli shemelachto l'issur* type two.

101. Is an electric cord muktzeh?
- If it is not connected to an appliance, it is a *kli shemelachto l'issur* type two.
- If it is connected to an appliance, it has the same laws as the appliance.

102. Is a watch muktzeh?
No. Although it is battery operated, it is working continually and is not switched off like other appliances.

103. What if the watch incorporates a calculator?
It is not muktzeh since the calculator is secondary to the watch.

104. What if the watch has stopped?
- If the watch is decorative and would be worn as jewelry, it is not muktzeh. This might apply to some ladies' watches.
- If the watch is not decorative and would not be worn as jewelry, it is *muktzeh machmas gufo* (category three). This applies to most men's watches.

105. What if it stopped while one was wearing it?

If the watch is muktzeh, one should remove it as soon as possible, preferably in an unusual way such as with one's teeth. If this happened outside and he does not wish to remove the watch for fear of theft, he should go to a safe place and remove it there. See also Question 442.

106. Is a cellphone muktzeh?

- If the alarm is set to ring, it is a *kli shemelachto l'issur* type one.
- If the alarm is not set or it has already rung, it is a *kli shemelachto l'issur* type two.

107. May one move it if the ringing alarm is disturbing?

Yes, this is considered as needing its place.

Chapter Five
Muktzeh Machmas Chisaron Kis

108. What is *muktzeh machmas chisaron kis*?

Literally, it means muktzeh due to potential monetary loss. This refers to an item whose use is severely limited by the owner out of fear of damage. If the owner would not permit its use on Shabbos, it is muktzeh.

109. What is an example?

A *shechita* knife. Although such a knife is theoretically suitable for cutting food, the owner would never permit this because the razor-sharp smooth edge might be damaged. Since *shechita* is forbidden on Shabbos, the knife has no use and is therefore *muktzeh machmas chisaron kis*.

110. What are the rules of *muktzeh machmas chisaron kis*?

It may not be moved directly even if it is needed for some permitted purpose or one needs to use the place where it is lying. It may only be moved in an indirect or unusual way if necessary. Contrast Question 60.

111. Are only expensive items included?

No. What is relevant is not the value of the item but rather the owner's attitude toward it. An expensive item that most people would not use on Shabbos but the owner would use is not muktzeh. On the other hand, even an inexpensive article that the owner would refuse to use on Shabbos is muktzeh. For example, a blank notebook or writing pad that one would not use for anything else is *muktzeh machmas chisaron kis*.

112. Does this apply to a single blank sheet?

- If the owner would not use it for anything else other than writing, it is *muktzeh machmas chisaron kis*.
- If the owner would not mind using it for other purposes, opinions differ regarding its status. According to some opinions, it is a *kli shemelachto l'issur* type one, and according to others it is not muktzeh at all.

113. What if a notebook is partially written in?

The notebook is considered as one unit, and the blank pages are insignificant compared to the written pages. Therefore, if it is permitted reading material, the entire notebook is not muktzeh. However, according to some opinions, it is preferable to avoid turning the blank pages.

114. What if a loose-leaf is partially written in?

The pages in a loose-leaf binder are considered as separate items since they are inserted or removed as needed. Therefore the written pages are not muktzeh (provided they may be read on Shabbos), and the blank pages are subject to the rules of Question 112.

115. Is a blank envelope *muktzeh machmas chisaron kis*?

No, it is a *kli shemelachto l'issur* type one. Although its primary use is for sealing a letter, people often use it as a bookmark or to hold photographs, etc.

116. Is wrapping paper muktzeh?

A roll is *muktzeh machmas gufo*, but a cut piece is not muktzeh.

117. Are important documents *muktzeh machmas chisaron kis*?

Yes, if they are valid and must be kept. For example: birth certificate, check book, contract, credit card, driving license, identity card, passport.

118. Is a *kesuba* muktzeh?

No, since one can study the laws of a *kesuba* from it. However, if it is framed and hung on the wall, it is muktzeh, see Question 120.

119. Are stamps muktzeh?

- An unused stamp is *muktzeh machmas chisaron kis*.
- A used stamp is *muktzeh machmas gufo* (category three).
- A collection of stamps whether used or unused is not muktzeh. However, rare and very valuable stamps are *muktzeh machmas chisaron kis*.

120. Is a framed picture muktzeh?

- If the owner has designated a fixed place for it and rarely moves it for fear of damage, it is *muktzeh machmas chisaron kis*. This is usually the case when it hangs on the wall.
- If the picture is often moved, it is not muktzeh. This is usually the case when it stands on a table or dresser.

121. May one straighten a wall picture that is crooked?

No, since it is muktzeh. If one is very disturbed, he could try to straighten it with his elbow (see Question 438).

122. What if the picture fell on the floor?

It is muktzeh whether or not it broke, and it may only be moved in an indirect or unusual way. See also Question 485.

123. Is a wall clock muktzeh?

Yes, it is *muktzeh machmas chisaron kis* and has the same laws as a wall picture.

124. What if an inexpensive picture is hung on the wall?

If the owner hung it there for convenience but not due to fear of damage, opinions differ whether it is *muktzeh machmas chisaron kis*.

125. Is a valuable ornament muktzeh?

- If the owner does not mind it being handled, it is not muktzeh.
- If the owner keeps it in a fixed place and does not allow it to be handled for fear of damage, it is *muktzeh machmas chisaron kis*. This might apply to articles of silver or crystal that are kept in a breakfront or an expensive artificial flower arrangement. However, if the owner would be prepared to use it on special occasions, it is not muktzeh.

126. Are Pesach utensils muktzeh during the year?

- If the owner would be prepared to use them in times of need, they are not muktzeh.
- If the owner would not be prepared to use them in times of need, they are still not muktzeh according to many opinions. According to some opinions, they are *muktzeh machmas chisaron kis*.

127. Are chametz utensils muktzeh on Pesach?

- Utensils used for hot foods or drinks are *muktzeh machmas chisaron kis* on Shabbos and Yom Tov of Pesach.
- Utensils used only for cold foods and drinks are not muktzeh.

128. Is merchandise muktzeh?

- Most people who sell items, whether in a store or from the house, would not usually take from their supply for their own use or to lend to other people. Since they are set aside for business, they are *muktzeh machmas chisaron kis*. This applies even to articles that are not usually muktzeh, such as clothing and tableware. See also next question for exceptions.
- If the owner would occasionally take from his stock to use or to lend, they are not *muktzeh machmas chisaron kis*. (Nevertheless, they might be muktzeh for other reasons, e.g. electric appliances, writing materials, and tools.)

129. Which items are exceptions?

- Food and drinks.
- *Sefarim*.

Since these items are always needed on Shabbos, they are not muktzeh even if they are set aside to be sold. Therefore, the owner may take from his stock for himself or for others if the need arises on Shabbos.

130. Are *esrogim* that are for sale muktzeh?

Yes, they are *muktzeh machmas chisaron kis*. Although they are a type of food, they are muktzeh since they are set aside for sale only and not for eating.

131. Is a bought *esrog* muktzeh?

- If the owner does not allow anyone to see or smell it, it is *muktzeh machmas chisaron kis* on Shabbos before or during Succos.
- If the owner allows people to see or smell it, it is not muktzeh.

132. Is a mezuza muktzeh?

No, since one can study the laws of mezuza from it.

133. What if a mezuza fell from the doorpost on Shabbos?

It is not muktzeh. Therefore, it must be picked up.

134. May it be returned to its place on the doorpost?

- If the mezuza case needs reattaching, this is forbidden.
- If the mezuza case is on the doorpost and the mezuza could be inserted, most opinions permit doing so.

135. Are there other examples of *muktzeh machmas chisaron kis*?

Yes. An item that one bought and decided definitely to return to the store is *muktzeh machmas chisaron kis*. This is because the buyer will not allow anyone to use the item since he must return it in perfect condition.

136. Is an intended gift muktzeh?

- If one intends to give it after Shabbos, it is *muktzeh machmas chisaron kis* since he does not want it to appear used.
- If one intends to give it on Shabbos, it is not muktzeh since it is prepared for that use.

Note: Giving a gift on Shabbos is subject to certain conditions. A Rav should be consulted.

137. Is a found article muktzeh?

A lost article that one found and hopes to return to its owner is not *muktzeh machmas chisaron kis*. Although one may not use the item, it is not muktzeh since it can be returned on Shabbos if the owner is discovered. This is assuming the item does not belong to one of the other categories of muktzeh.

Chapter Six
Muktzeh Machmas Gufo

138. What is *muktzeh machmas gufo*?

It means something that is muktzeh because it is useless. The most basic type is an item that is inherently useless, i.e. by its very nature it is usually useless even on a weekday. For example, garbage. However, this category also includes items that are useful on weekdays but are useless on Shabbos. For example, money. There are also three general subsections under the heading of *muktzeh machmas gufo*:

• *Muktzeh machmas issur* - an item whose use involves a prohibition. For example, a garment of *shaatnez*. See Chapter Eight.

• *Muktzeh machmas mitzvah* - an item that is reserved for fulfilling a mitzvah. For example, succah decorations. See Chapter Nine.

• *Nolad* - an item that came into existence on Shabbos. E.g. a newly laid egg. See Chapter Ten.

139. What are the rules of *muktzeh machmas gufo*?

It may not be moved directly even if it is needed for some permitted purpose or one needs to use the place where it is lying. It may only be moved in an indirect or unusual way if necessary. Contrast Question 60.

140. What are examples of inherently useless items?

Sticks, stones, earth, dirt, sand, leaves, trees, inedible food (e.g. flour, raw potatoes, see Question 156), broken utensils (see Question 188), garbage, animals, birds, fish (see Question 218). All these are *muktzeh machmas gufo*.

141. What are examples of items that are useless on Shabbos?

Ball of string, ball of thread, ball of wool, bleach, cosmetics, creams, deodorant stick, glue, money, most medicines (see Questions 174-175), paint, roll of dental floss, roll of foil, roll of toilet paper, scotch tape, shoe polish, silver polish, staples, toothpaste, washing powder. All these are *muktzeh machmas gufo*.

142. Why are these not classified as *kli shemelachto l'issur*?

A *kli shemelachto l'issur* is a utensil that can be used repeatedly to do a particular job. The items listed above are not considered as utensils since they are consumed through use. For example, a paintbrush is a utensil since it can be used many times, whereas paint is not a utensil since it is used up while painting.

143. Why is money not a utensil?

Although money is not consumed through use, it is nevertheless not considered a utensil. This is because the way one uses it is only by transfering it from one person to another.

144. Could a *muktzeh machmas gufo* item be converted into a utensil?

Yes, through a procedure called 'designation'. For example, a rock could be made non-muktzeh by designating it as a doorstop. The details of this procedure will be explained in the next chapter.

145. Is a candle *muktzeh machmas gufo*?

- A lit candle is a *bosis* to the flame.
- An unlit candle is *muktzeh machmas gufo* according to some opinions, but it is a *kli shemelachto l'issur* type two according to other opinions.

146. Are matches *muktzeh machmas gufo*?

According to some opinions, they are *muktzeh machmas gufo*.

147. Is soap muktzeh?

- A bar of soap is muktzeh since its use involves the *melacha* of *memarei'ach* (smoothing). According to most opinions, it is *muktzeh machmas gufo*.
- Liquid soap is not muktzeh and may be used on Shabbos (according to some opinions, it must be very diluted).

Therefore, if a bar of soap falls into a sink, one should not pick it up. If it is in the way, one may remove it in an indirect way, e.g. with a spoon.

148. Why is a tree muktzeh?

A tree is *muktzeh machmas gufo* since it has no permitted use on Shabbos. This is because *Chazal* instituted a decree against using a tree due to a concern that one might break off a branch or leaves. Forbidden uses include:
- Climbing a tree.
- Leaning on it.
- Placing items on it (e.g. a jacket).
- Removing items from it (e.g. a stuck ball).

Since a tree is muktzeh, one must not move its leaves or branches. See also Question 465.

Note: There are other forbidden uses, but the subject is beyond the scope of this *sefer*.

149. May one sit on tree roots or branches?

One may sit on roots or branches that are lower than three *tefachim* from the ground (24cm) since they are considered part of the ground. This is permitted even if the roots or branches bend. Contrast Question 445.

150. Is grass muktzeh?

No. One may sit or lie on grass even if this involves touching it, but care should be taken not to detach a blade of grass. Detached blades of grass (e.g. on one's shoe) are *muktzeh machmas gufo* and may not be moved directly with one's hand. See Question 507.

151. Is a growing flower muktzeh?

- If its stem is woody, it is considered like a tree and is muktzeh.
- If its stem is soft and pliable, it is not muktzeh. Therefore, one may carefully bend it toward oneself in order to smell its fragrance.

152. Is a plant in a flowerpot muktzeh?

This is a complex issue depending on many factors. Therefore, it is preferable to make a general rule and consider all potted plants muktzeh.

153. Are cut flowers muktzeh?

No. Even if they are in a vase of water, they are not muktzeh and may be moved.

Note: Cut flowers may not be put into water on Shabbos.

154. Are artificial flowers muktzeh?

No. This includes dried flower arrangements, plastic and silk flowers, artificial grass, etc. See also Question 125.

Inedible Food

155. Why is inedible food muktzeh?
Since it is forbidden to cook on Shabbos, the food is useless.

156. What are examples?
Dough; flour; yeast; raw: beans, beets, chicken, fish, meat, noodles, quince, potatoes, and rice. If such foods are in the refrigerator or freezer, one must take care not to move them directly when putting in or taking out other food.

157. Aren't some of these foods fit for animals?
- In a city where animals are not commonly found, it is irrelevant that they could eat such foods.
- In a city where animals are commonly found or if one owns an animal, opinions differ whether this is relevant. According to some opinions, the food is still considered useless since it has been set aside for human consumption, and it is highly unlikely that one would give it to an animal. According to other opinions, the food is not muktzeh since theoretically one could give it to an animal. One may be lenient in times of need.

158. Is pet food muktzeh?
If one owns a pet, its food is not muktzeh since it is prepared for use.

159. Could raw meat be chewed?

In the days of old, it was not unusual for some people to chew raw meat, and therefore it was not muktzeh. Nowadays, such a practice is extremely rare and therefore raw meat is subject to the rules of Question 157.

160. Isn't raw fish eaten today in sushi?

In many places certain types of fish are eaten raw on their own (sashimi) or in a dish (sushi). In such places those types of fish are not muktzeh even for people who would not eat it like that.

161. Are raw eggs muktzeh?

In the days of old, it was not unusual for people to eat raw eggs, and therefore they were not muktzeh. Nowadays, most people will not eat raw eggs due to health concerns, but some people still would. According to most opinions, they are not muktzeh.

162. Is ground coffee muktzeh?

No, since one could use it to make iced coffee that does not need cooking.

163. Are tea-bags muktzeh?

No, since one could use them to make iced tea that does not need cooking. There is also a permitted way to make hot tea with tea-bags (see Guidelines to Bishul, Question 121).

164. Is a sealed can of edible food muktzeh?

No, since there are permitted ways to open the can.

165. Is a can opener muktzeh?

It is a *kli shemelachto l'issur* type one, since its primary use is to open cans in a forbidden way. Nevertheless, it may be used to open a bottle or to open a can in a permitted way when necessary.

166. Is a sealed bottle of wine muktzeh?

No, since there are permitted ways to open it.

167. Is a corkscrew muktzeh?

No, since its use is permitted.

168. Is edible frozen food muktzeh?

No, since it could be defrosted and eaten on Shabbos. This applies even close to the end of Shabbos when there does not remain sufficient time to defrost it. Compare Question 516.

169. Is an unripe fruit or vegetable muktzeh?

- If it is partially ripe, it is not muktzeh.
- If it is completely unripe, it is muktzeh. However, if it ripens and becomes edible on Shabbos, it ceases to be muktzeh. See Question 455.

170. Are food leftovers muktzeh?

- Sizeable pieces that are sometimes saved by people are not muktzeh even if one wishes to discard them.
- Small scraps that are usually discarded are muktzeh. Nevertheless, one may carry them on the plate and scrape them into the garbage since this is indirect movement. See Question 428.
- Small scraps that a child has left are not muktzeh if a parent is interested in eating them.

171. What if the scraps of food are fit for animals?

If one owns such an animal or there are many people in the city who own such animals, the scraps are not muktzeh. Otherwise, they are muktzeh. Contrast Question 157.

172. Are crumbs of bread muktzeh?

- During the meal, they are not muktzeh since people sometimes eat them.
- After *bensching*, they are muktzeh since they are usually discarded.

Therefore, if one wishes to brush the crumbs off the table by hand, one should do so before *bensching*. After *bensching*, one may gather the crumbs with a tissue, knife, etc. and brush them onto a plate rather than into one's hand. See Question 215.

173. Are crumbs of cake or biscuits muktzeh?

No.

Medicines

174. Are medicines muktzeh?

Generally, medicines are *muktzeh machmas gufo*. Since most people do not require medicines, they are not prepared for use on Shabbos and are therefore muktzeh.

175. Which medicines are not muktzeh?

- Medicines that one knew before Shabbos that they would be needed on Shabbos. For example: a person takes daily medications or one began a course of medication before Shabbos that must not be interrupted.
- Medicines for common ailments even if there is no one sick in the house. For example: aspirin, paracetamol, Tylenol, Advil.

Note: There are restrictions regarding who is permitted to take medicine on Shabbos. Therefore, in times of need a Rav should be consulted.

176. May such medicines be handled by anyone?

Yes. Since they are not muktzeh, they may be handled even by a healthy person.

177. Are medicines in a *gemach* muktzeh?

No. Since it is quite possible that someone in the neighborhood will need one of the medicines, they are considered prepared for use. The same applies to medicines in a hospital, clinic, or pharmacy.

178. What if a person unexpectedly needs medicine on Shabbos?

- If it is a commonly needed medicine, it is not muktzeh.
- If it is not a commonly needed medicine, he should try to obtain it from a *gemach* since such medicine is not muktzeh.

179. What if he or a neighbor owns the required medicine?

The medicine is muktzeh, but the sick person is permitted to take the required dose. Since the medicine is muktzeh, it should be handled only as minimally as possible whether by the patient or by a healthy person. Preferably, it should be moved in a slightly unusual way. If the medicine was removed from a carton, it may not be returned there since the carton is a muktzeh *bosis* and may not be handled.

180. May the medicine be placed in a refrigerator?

After the patient has taken a dose, the medicine must be put down and not moved again until a further dose is required. However, it may be placed in a refrigerator if this is necessary. Similarly, it may be moved to keep it out of the reach of children. See Question 489.

181. Are vitamins muktzeh?

This depends on the reason why the person wishes to take the vitamin:

- If he is ill to the extent that he needs medication, he may take the vitamin on Shabbos and it is not muktzeh.
- If he feels slightly weak, he may not take the vitamin on Shabbos and it is *muktzeh machmas gufo*.
- If he is healthy and desires extra strength or protection, opinions differ whether he may take the vitamin on Shabbos and whether it is muktzeh.
- If he is healthy and uses the vitamin as a substitute for regular food, he may take it on Shabbos and it is not muktzeh.

The same applies to supplements such as iron and calcium.

Note: It is often possible to avoid taking vitamins on Shabbos by taking them just before and just after Shabbos. In some cases, skipping one day will cause no harm. A doctor should be consulted.

182. Are children's vitamins muktzeh?

No. Vitamins may be given to all children up to the age of nine or ten according to their need.

183. Are sleeping pills muktzeh?

In certain circumstances, it is permitted to take sleeping pills on Shabbos after consulting a Rav. If such a situation is anticipated before Shabbos, the pills are not muktzeh.

184. What if the required medicine is surrounded by other types?

When selecting the required medicine, one must take care not to directly move other medicines that are muktzeh. If necessary, they may be moved aside indirectly, such as with a knife.

Note: Extreme care is needed to avoid the *melacha* of *borer*. Therefore, the required medicine may only be selected shortly before it is to be taken, and other medication may not be totally removed from the mixture. See Guidelines to Borer, Questions 64 and 65.

185. Is a thermometer muktzeh?

- A digital thermometer is muktzeh since it may not be used on Shabbos.
- A non-digital thermometer is not muktzeh since it may be used on Shabbos.

186. Are ear plugs muktzeh?

- Wax ear plugs are muktzeh since they may not be used on Shabbos.
- Sponge ear plugs are not muktzeh since they may be used on Shabbos.

187. Are Band-Aids muktzeh?

No, since they may be used on Shabbos.

Broken Utensils

188. When are broken utensils muktzeh?

If a utensil breaks to the extent that the pieces are completely unusable, they are *muktzeh machmas gufo*. For example, a china plate that falls on the floor and breaks into two or more pieces. One may not pick up the pieces by hand but may discard them using a broom and a dustpan (see Question 428). If the broken pieces might cause injury to someone, they may be moved even directly (see Question 485). Similarly, if an article no longer functions, it is *muktzeh machmas gufo*. E.g. a broken cellphone. See also Question 230.

189. Does it matter whether it breaks before or on Shabbos?

No, there is no difference.

190. What if the owner intends to repair the broken item?

It is still muktzeh since it is presently useless.

191. What if some of the pieces are usable?

In most cases, the pieces that are usable are not muktzeh, but the pieces that are not usable are muktzeh. For example, if a china plate falls and becomes chipped, the plate is not muktzeh but the chipped fragment is muktzeh. In certain cases, a special decree of muktzeh applies to prevent one from trying to repair the item on Shabbos. See Questions 272-279. See also Question 343.

192. What if the owner does not want to keep the chipped plate?

It is not muktzeh since it is still usable. He may pick it up and discard it.

193. Does it become muktzeh after he has discarded it?

- If he threw the broken item into the garbage and then changed his mind, he may retrieve it since it is still usable. This applies even if it broke before Shabbos and he discarded it on Shabbos.
- If it broke before Shabbos and he discarded it before Shabbos, it is muktzeh.

194. What if most people would discard such a broken item?

According to most opinions, it is muktzeh as soon as it breaks whether the owner wishes to keep it or discard it. For example, if a cup falls and the handle breaks off, most people would throw the cup away despite its being theoretically usable.

195. Is a cracked disposable cup muktzeh?

Yes. Although it is theoretically usable to hold small pieces of garbage such as pits, everyone throws away such a cup and therefore it is muktzeh. Care must be taken not to pick up a cracked cup when clearing the table. See also Question 496.

Garbage

196. What is included in garbage?

Common examples are: bones, inedible pits and seeds, inedible peels, candy wrappers, destroyed packages, leftover scraps of food (see Question 170), moldy food, shells, used diaper (but see Question 492). All these items are *muktzeh machmas gufo*.

197. What if there is food attached to a bone?

The bone is not muktzeh if there is food attached to it that people would generally be interested in eating. Compare Question 49.

198. What if a bone contains marrow?

It is not muktzeh.

199. What if there is food attached to an inedible pit?

The pit is not muktzeh if there is food attached to it that people would generally be interested in eating.

200. What if there is an edible seed inside a pit?

The pit is muktzeh since people do not usually eat the inner seed.

201. Which pits and seeds are edible?

Melon, watermelon, sunflower, and pumpkin seeds are edible and therefore not muktzeh.

202. Are apple and pear pits edible?

No, and therefore they are muktzeh.

203. Are apricot pits muktzeh?

Some children play games with these pits. If the pits were separated from the fruit before Shabbos and designated for play, they are not muktzeh. However, pits that were separated on Shabbos are muktzeh since designation is not effective on Shabbos (see Question 228).

204. May one remove a bone or pit from the mouth?

- If there is still food in the mouth, one may remove the bone or pit by hand.
- If there is no food in the mouth, one should spit the bone or pit onto a plate or into a tissue or napkin. If one feels this to be repulsive to oneself or to other people, he may remove it by hand.

205. Which peels are edible?

Apple, carrot, peach, pear, plum, radish. Such peels are not muktzeh even after they have been removed from the fruit or vegetable since they are often eaten together.

206. Which peels are inedible?

Avocado, banana, clementine, garlic, grapefruit, lemon, melon, onion, orange, pineapple, watermelon. Such peels are muktzeh.

207. What if there is food attached to the peel?

The peel is not muktzeh if there is food attached to it that people would generally be interested in eating.

208. What if the peels are edible to animals?

If the peels are inedible to humans but edible to animals, they are not muktzeh in two situations:
- Many people in that city own animals that would eat such peels.
- The owner of the peels possesses an animal that would eat them.

Otherwise, the peels are muktzeh. Compare Question 157. The same applies to bones and pits. See also Question 343.

209. Why can one peel a fruit or vegetable if the peel is muktzeh?

While the peel is still attached to the food it is not muktzeh, but as soon as it becomes detached it is muktzeh. The same applies when shelling nuts and eggs and when eating sunflower seeds or similar foods. Nevertheless, one does not need to drop the peel or shell immediately onto a plate but may carry it to the garbage bin. See also Question 505.

210. Why are candy wrappers muktzeh?

After the wrapper has been removed it is useless, and therefore it is muktzeh like an inedible peel. The same applies to the paper of cupcakes, petit fours, ices, etc.

211. Is a used disposable plastic cup muktzeh?

No. Although most people throw it away, it is not a broken item and is sometimes reused after rinsing. See also Question 195.

212. What if it was thrown into the garbage?
- If it was discarded before Shabbos, it is muktzeh.
- If it was discarded on Shabbos, opinions differ whether it is muktzeh.

213. Are used disposable plastic plates and cutlery muktzeh?
- Before they are discarded, they are not muktzeh according to most opinions since they could be rinsed and reused.
- If they were discarded before Shabbos, they are muktzeh.
- If they were discarded on Shabbos, opinions differ whether they are muktzeh.

The same applies to empty soda bottles.

214. Is an empty yoghurt container muktzeh?
- According to many opinions, it is muktzeh even before it is discarded since everyone considers it as garbage.
- According to some opinions, the rules of the previous question apply.

These rules apply to other similar used items such as empty cheese containers, empty drink cartons, used paper cups and plates.

215. How can one clear garbage off the table?

- One may scrape garbage, leftovers, etc. with a knife into a regular bowl or plate, and take it to tilt out into the bin, see Question 428.
- One may remove the tablecloth and shake the garbage into the bin.
- If the table was covered with a disposable tablecloth, one may roll up the cloth with everything in it and discard it all.
- If there is a large quantity of garbage on the table and one is repulsed by it, one may remove it directly, see Question 496.

216. Isn't the disposable tablecloth also garbage?

No, since it continues to be useful to hold all the garbage on it.

217. Is used *nagel vasser* muktzeh?

No. Although the custom is to throw it out, nevertheless it is technically usable and therefore not muktzeh. The same applies to used *mayim acharonim*.

Animals

218. Why are animals muktzeh?
All animals, birds, fish, insects etc. are muktzeh since one may not slaughter them, ride on them, or use them in any way.

219. Are pets muktzeh?
Yes, since playing with them or looking at them is not considered as using them.

220. What if a pet jumps on one's lap?
He may remain seated without touching the pet. If he wants to remove it, he may stand up and allow the pet to jump off.

221. May one stroke a pet?
It is preferable not to do so.

222. What if an ant or insect is on the table or counter?
One may blow it off or gently push it off with a tissue, cloth, etc. Care must be taken not to kill the creature.

223. Is a seeing eye dog muktzeh?
Opinions differ about this, and a Rav should be consulted. In any event, the blind person may certainly hold the harness and be led by the dog.
Note: Regarding walking with the dog outdoors where there is no *eiruv*, a Rav should be consulted.

224. Is a bird cage muktzeh?

- If there was a bird in the cage at the beginning of Shabbos, the cage is a muktzeh *bosis*.
- If there was no bird in the cage at the beginning of Shabbos, the cage is a *kli shemelachto l'issur* type one. See Question 53.

The same applies to a basket designated for a pet to sleep in.

Note: When a bird is inside its cage, it is forbidden to close the open door due to the *melacha* of trapping.

225. Is an aquarium muktzeh?

- According to most opinions, it is a muktzeh *bosis*.
- According to some opinions, it is a non-muktzeh ornament. However, if one rarely moves it due to fear of damage, it is *muktzeh machmas chisaron kis*.

The same applies to a fish bowl.

226. Is a spider web muktzeh?

Yes.

Chapter Seven
Designation

227. Could a muktzeh item be changed to become non-muktzeh?

Yes, through a procedure known as 'designation'. The concept is to convert an otherwise useless item into a usable utensil by designating it for a specific purpose.

228. When should this be done?

Designation must be done before Shabbos. Since an item that was muktzeh at the beginning of Shabbos remains muktzeh for the entire day, designation on Shabbos is ineffective. See Question 448.

229. How is designation done?

This depends on whether or not people normally designate that type of item for that intended use.

230. What are examples?

- It is unusual to designate a plank of wood as a bat for ball games.
- It is usual to designate a rock as a doorstop, a blank sheet of paper as a bookmark, and a broken telephone as a toy.

231. What are the rules for an unusual type of designation?

In this case, there are two ways to designate:
1. Decide to use the item permanently for that purpose.
2. Make a physical change to the item to prepare it for use.

232. With the first method must the decision be verbalized?

No, it is sufficient to make a mental decision.

233. What if one knows that he will eventually discard the item?

This method of designation must be permanent, i.e. he intends to use the item indefinitely. If he plans from the outset to discard it after some time, the designation is not effective and the item remains muktzeh. In this situation, it is recommended to use the second method of designation.

234. With the second method must the designation be permanent?

No. If the item is changed physically, it is considered non-muktzeh even if it will be used for only one Shabbos. For example, a plank of wood that one wants to use as a bat could be cut to shape or sanded smooth.

235. What are the rules for a normal type of designation?

The above two methods are certainly effective. According to some opinions, one may decide to use the item temporarily for a particular purpose without making a physical change. This may be relied upon in times of need.

236. How does this apply to using a rock as a doorstop?

- If one wishes to use a rock as a doorstop permanently, it is sufficient to designate it mentally as such.
- If one wishes to use a rock as a doorstop temporarily (e.g. he intends to have the door fixed after Shabbos), he should preferably make a physical change to the rock, such as removing the jagged or sharp edges. In times of need, it is sufficient to designate it mentally.

237. How does this apply to using a sheet of paper as a bookmark?

- If this is permanent, mental designation is sufficient.
- If this is temporary, one should preferably fold the sheet into a narrow strip.

238. What if one began to use the item before Shabbos without designating it?

- If this is a normal type of usage, the item has become non-muktzeh.
- If this is an unusual type of usage, the item remains muktzeh despite the fact that one began to use it for that purpose. However, if one was using it regularly in that way, it has become non-muktzeh according to some opinions.

239. May a designated item be used for other purposes?

Yes. Once a muktzeh item has been designated for a specific purpose it becomes non-muktzeh, and it may be used for other needs. For example, if a stone was designated as a doorstop, it may be used as a nutcracker.

240. Can a child designate an item?

- If it was designated through a decision, this is not effective and the item remains muktzeh.
- If it was designated through an action, this is effective and the item is non-muktzeh.

For example, if a child collected pebbles and put them into his toy box, they have become non-muktzeh toys.

241. What if a gentile designated one of his muktzeh items?

This is not effective and the item remains muktzeh. For example, a gentile designated a rock from his garden as a doorstop. The rock remains muktzeh for a Jew.

242. Is designation effective for *muktzeh machmas chisaron kis*?

Yes. The same methods of designation for *muktzeh machmas gufo* are effective for *muktzeh machmas chisaron kis*. For example, if a person decided to keep unused stamps as part of his stamp collection, they are no longer *muktzeh machmas chisaron kis* (see Question 117).

243. Is designation effective for a *kli shemelachto l'issur*?

Yes. For example, if a person decides before Shabbos to use a pot as a storage container and no longer for cooking, it becomes non-muktzeh.

Chapter Eight
Muktzeh Machmas Issur

244. What is *muktzeh machmas issur*?
It is an item that is forbidden to use whether by the Torah or Rabbinically. Due to the prohibition, the item is deemed useless and is classified as a special type of *muktzeh machmas gufo*. This category of muktzeh is sub-divided into two groups:
1. Items that are forbidden to use even on a weekday.
2. Items that are forbidden to use on Shabbos due to a special decree.

245. What are the rules of *muktzeh machmas issur*?
It may not be moved directly even if it is needed for some permitted purpose or one needs to use the place where it is lying. It may only be moved in an indirect or unusual way if necessary. Contrast Question 60.

246. What are examples in the first group?
- *Tevel*.
- Certain meat and milk mixtures.
- Wine of idolatry.
- Chametz on Pesach.
- A garment containing *shaatnez*.

247. What is *tevel*?

There are two types of *tevel*:
- Produce grown in *Eretz Yisroel* (fruits, vegetables, etc.) that has not been tithed.
- Baked goods (bread, cake, etc.) made in *Eretz Yisroel* from which *challah* has not been separated.

248. Why is *tevel* muktzeh?

It is forbidden to separate tithes or *challah* on Shabbos since this is considered a type of repairing. Since *tevel* must not be eaten by a Jew, gentile, or an animal, it is useless and therefore muktzeh. See also Question 519.

249. What if one does not know whether the food was tithed?

It is muktzeh since it might be *tevel* and must be tithed. For example, produce bought in a store that does not have reliable supervision.

250. What if one mistakenly tithed on Shabbos?

Although this is wrong, the food is no longer muktzeh.

251. What if a person usually tithes food with a hechsher?

A hechsher on food grown in *Eretz Yisroel* testifies that it has been tithed. Nevertheless, many people tithe such food themselves as an extra precaution to ensure that they will not eat *tevel*. If they have not yet tithed the food, it is not muktzeh on Shabbos since it is really edible and they are only acting more strictly.

252. Is the tithed portion muktzeh?

When tithing food, the separated portion is called *terumah*. Nowadays, no one is permitted to eat *terumah* and it must be disposed of. If one did not dispose of it before Shabbos, it is *muktzeh machmas issur*. The same applies to the separated piece of *challah*.

253. What if *challah* was not separated from baked goods in *Chutz La'aretz*?

Although such food is not *tevel*, the custom is not to eat it before *challah* is separated. If it is needed on Shabbos, one may eat from it provided a piece is put aside until after Shabbos when *challah* must be separated from it. Therefore, such food is not muktzeh whether or not one will eat it on Shabbos.

254. Is the piece put aside muktzeh?

No, since one could eat some of it and leave aside a smaller piece.

255. Which meat and milk mixtures are muktzeh?

If meat and milk were cooked together, whether deliberately or accidentally, one is forbidden by the Torah to have any benefit whatsoever from the mixture. Since it must be disposed of, it is useless, and therefore it is *muktzeh machmas issur*.

256. Which meat and milk mixtures are not muktzeh?

If chicken and milk were cooked together or if cold meat and milk were mixed together, one is forbidden Rabbinically to eat the mixture. However, one may benefit from it, such as by giving it to a gentile or an animal. Since the mixture may be used, it is not muktzeh.

257. Is treif food muktzeh?

Aside from meat and milk mixtures, all treif food is only forbidden to eat but benefit is permitted. Therefore, it is not useless and is not muktzeh.

258. What is wine of idolatry?

If wine was used for any form of idol worship, one is forbidden by the Torah to have any benefit from it. Since it must be disposed of, it is useless, and therefore it is *muktzeh machmas issur*.

259. What if a gentile touched wine?

Chazal prohibited drinking uncooked wine or grape juice that was touched or moved by a gentile. Opinions differ whether it is also forbidden to benefit from it, and one should be strict in this matter except in difficult circumstances. Therefore, it is considered useless on Shabbos and is *muktzeh machmas issur*.

260. Why is chametz on Pesach muktzeh?

It is forbidden to have any benefit from chametz on Pesach. Therefore, it is useless and it is *muktzeh machmas issur*. This applies even to chametz that one sold to a gentile.

261. What if one finds chametz in the house on Pesach?

Although one is usually permitted to move muktzeh in an indirect or unusual way when necessary (see Chapter Thirteen), chametz is an exception and may not be moved at all. If one finds chametz on Shabbos or Yom Tov during Pesach, he must cover it until after Shabbos or Yom Tov and burn it immediately after *Havdalah*.

262. What if *erev Pesach* falls on Shabbos?

Chametz may not be eaten after the fourth hour of the day. However, it is not forbidden to benefit from it until after the fifth hour, by which time all chametz must be disposed of. After that time, any remaining chametz becomes useless and is *muktzeh machmas issur*.

263. Are *kitniyos* muktzeh on Pesach?

Kitniyos are certain vegetables and seeds that may not be eaten on Pesach according to the Ashkenazic custom. They are not muktzeh when owned by Ashkenazim since they may be eaten by Sephardim. (If they are raw and inedible, they are muktzeh on Shabbos but not on Yom Tov, see Question 515.)

264. Is *chadash* muktzeh?

Chadash is food made from grain that was planted after Pesach and harvested before the following Pesach. Such food may not be eaten until the third day of Pesach. However one may benefit from it, and therefore it is not muktzeh.

265. Is edible food muktzeh on Yom Kippur?

No, since it may be given to children and dangerously sick people.

266. Are leather shoes muktzeh on Yom Kippur?

According to most opinions, they are not muktzeh since they may be worn in certain circumstances.

267. Why is a garment containing *shaatnez* muktzeh?

Since it is forbidden to wear *shaatnez*, the garment is useless and is therefore *muktzeh machmas issur*.

268. What if the garment might contain *shaatnez*?

If there is an obligation to check the garment for *shaatnez*, it is muktzeh since one may not wear it.

269. Is a tallis without *tzitzis* muktzeh?

No. It may be worn by someone other than the owner because a borrowed tallis does not need *tzitzis*. The same applies to a tallis whose *tzitzis* became *passul*. The same rules apply to a *tallis katan*.

270. Is a new utensil muktzeh if it requires immersion in a mikveh?

No, since it may be used by giving it to a gentile and borrowing it back.

271. Is a utensil that became treif muktzeh?

If it is suitable for another use besides food, it is not muktzeh. For example: to store paper clips, flowers, etc. Otherwise it is *muktzeh machmas issur*.

Special Decrees

272. Which items are muktzeh due to a special decree?

In certain cases, a usable item is muktzeh since its use might lead a person to do a *melacha*. *Chazal* enacted a special decree to make it muktzeh in order to safeguard against such a mistake. For example:

1. A partially broken utensil is muktzeh if one might be tempted to repair it and transgress the *melacha* of *makeh bepatish* (repairing).
2. A wet garment is muktzeh if one might be tempted to wring it out and transgress the *melacha* of *melabein* (laundering).
3. Fruit that fell off a tree on Shabbos is muktzeh since one might be tempted to pick one from the tree and transgress the *melacha* of *kotzeir* (harvesting).
4. Juice that seeped from fruit on Shabbos is muktzeh if one might be tempted to squeeze the fruit intentionally and transgress the *melacha* of *dosh* (threshing).

273. What is an example of the first case?

If the leg of a table, chair, couch, etc. became detached and could be reattached, both the piece of furniture and the leg are muktzeh since one might be tempted to make a repair. Therefore, it is forbidden to use the table, chair, couch, etc. by propping up the corner with some article to replace the missing leg.

274. What if the leg broke before Shabbos?

- If the furniture was used before Shabbos in its broken state, it is not muktzeh since one demonstrated that he is not anxious to repair it.
- If the furniture was not used before Shabbos in its broken state, it is muktzeh.

275. What if the repair needs skill?

If the repair can only be done by a craftsman, the decree does not apply. The item of furniture is not muktzeh if it is still usable, albeit with difficulty, but the broken leg is muktzeh since it is useless. The same applies if the leg is broken beyond repair and must be replaced.

276. Is the rule the same for a craftsman?

Yes, and the decree does not apply. Although he is capable of repairing his own broken furniture, the decree is standardized and only applies when the repair can be done by an unskilled person.

277. What if the detached part is not essential?

If a non-essential part became detached from an article, the decree does not apply even if it is easy to repair. Since the article is still perfectly usable, there is no concern that one might inadvertently repair it. For example, if the door or doorknob of a small cabinet, dresser, etc. became detached, the piece of furniture is not muktzeh since it is perfectly usable without a door or doorknob. Similarly, if an arm-rest became detached from a chair, the chair is not muktzeh.

278. Is the detached part muktzeh?
- If it is usable in some way, it is not muktzeh.
- If it is unusable and one intends to discard it, it is muktzeh.
- If it is unusable and one intends to reattach it, opinions differ whether it is muktzeh.

279. What if a craftsman is needed to fix it?

In this case, the detached part is muktzeh even if one intends to have it reattached.

280. What if the handle fell off a door of a house?

The handle is muktzeh since the rules above only apply to parts detached from small movable articles. If part of a building became detached, it is muktzeh since it is not considered a utensil. The same applies to objects attached to a building and to large heavy objects that are rarely moved, such as a refrigerator.

281. What are other examples?
- A handle that fell off a closet door.
- A faucet knob that came off.
- A plastic suction hook that fell off the side of a refrigerator.

All these items are muktzeh.

282. What if such items are loose and fall off regularly?
They are not muktzeh. Opinions differ whether they may be reattached loosely. Compare Question 285.

283. What if a wheel fell off a four wheeled stroller?
- If a craftsman is needed to reattach it, the stroller is not muktzeh but the wheel is muktzeh.
- If the wheel can be reattached easily, opinions differ whether this is considered an essential part of the stroller.
  - According to some opinions, it is comparable to a table with a broken leg. Therefore, both the stroller and the wheel are muktzeh due to the special decree.
  - According to other opinions, it is comparable to a cabinet without a door. Therefore, the stroller is not muktzeh, and opinions differ whether the wheel is muktzeh (see Questions 277 and 278).

284. How could such a muktzeh stroller be brought home?

If one wishes to be strict and consider the stroller muktzeh, he could bring it home in an indirect or unusual way. For example, he may hook his arm around the handles and pull it. The wheel may be kicked home.

285. What if the wheel falls off regularly?

If the wheel has become loose and falls off regularly, it may be reattached loosely on Shabbos since this is not considered a repair. In this case, the decree does not apply, and both the stroller and the wheel are not muktzeh.

286. What if a wheel fell off a three wheeled stroller?

If the wheel has become loose and falls off regularly, it may be reattached loosely on Shabbos. Otherwise, the wheel may not be reattached, and both the stroller and wheel are muktzeh.

287. What if a screw fell out of the frame of eyeglasses?

- If the screw is loose and falls out regularly, it may be put back loosely and nothing is muktzeh.
- If the screw does not fall out regularly but one does not have a suitable screwdriver to repair it, the glasses are not muktzeh and the screw is muktzeh. Similarly, if the screw is lost, the glasses are not muktzeh.

- If the screw does not fall out regularly and one has a suitable screwdriver to repair it, opinions differ whether the decree applies since the broken glasses could still be worn although with some difficulty. It is suggested to deliberately lose the screw by throwing it away (indirectly). The glasses are then not muktzeh according to all opinions.

288. May one temporarily fix the frame with a safety pin?

In the cases where the glasses are not muktzeh one may do this.

289. What if a lens fell out of the glasses?

- If it is loose and falls out regularly, it may be put back loosely and nothing is muktzeh.
- If it does not fall out regularly but a craftsman is needed to repair it, the glasses are not muktzeh. The lens is muktzeh unless it could be used like a magnifying glass.
- If it does not fall out regularly and one could reattach it, the decree applies. Therefore, both the glasses and the lens are muktzeh.

290. May one continue to wear muktzeh eyeglasses?

No. They must be removed immediately in an indirect or unusual way if possible, e.g. with a spoon or by shaking one's head. If they might be lost or damaged there, he may walk to a safe place and remove them there.

291. What if a button fell off a garment?

- The garment is not muktzeh since the button is not an essential part.
- If one intends to discard the button, the button is muktzeh.
- If the button is a type that could be attached to the garment with a safety pin, it is not muktzeh. It is permitted to fix it temporarily like that if one wishes.
- If the button cannot be attached with a safety pin and one intends to sew it after Shabbos, opinions differ whether it is muktzeh.

292. What if a broom-head fell off its stick?

- If it is loose and falls off regularly, one may repair it loosely and neither part is muktzeh.
- If it does not fall off regularly, the stick is muktzeh. Opinions differ whether the broom-head is muktzeh since it could be used independently with some difficulty.

Wet Garments

293. When is a wet garment muktzeh?

As explained in Question 272, a wet garment is muktzeh if there is a temptation to wring it out. This decree applies only if all the following conditions are fulfilled:

- The garment is very wet.
- The absorbed liquid cleans the garment.
- One is not wearing the garment.

294. What is meant by very wet?

This means that if one touches the garment and then touches a dry surface, the surface would become wet. This is a sufficient degree of wetness that might tempt a person to wring out the garment. If the garment is just damp or only slightly wet, it is not muktzeh since it is unlikely that one would try to squeeze it. Nevertheless, squeezing it is still forbidden.

295. What if only part of the garment is very wet?

The garment is muktzeh if the wet area is significant. For example, the cuff of a shirt.

296. Which liquids are considered as cleansers?

- Water even if slightly dirty.
- White wine or vinegar.

A garment that became very wet with either of these liquids is muktzeh. However, a garment that is very wet from spilled soup, juice, oil, red wine, etc. is not muktzeh since wringing it is pointless and there is no temptation to do so. Nevertheless, squeezing it is still forbidden.

297. What if one is wearing a wet garment?

If water spilled onto one's clothes or he was caught in a rainstorm, he may continue to wear the wet clothes and they are not muktzeh. Nevertheless, it is still forbidden to squeeze them.

298. Should he change clothing as soon as possible?

There is no obligation to do so.

299. Are the clothes muktzeh when he removes them?

Yes. Therefore, he should remove them in a place where he is able to put them down immediately in order to minimize handling muktzeh.

300. May he wear them again later?

- If the garment is no longer very wet (see Question 294), it is no longer muktzeh and may be worn.
- If the garment is still very wet, he may not wear it unless he has nothing else suitable. For example, a person got caught in the rain on the way to a friend's house and hung his wet jacket there. If he needs to wear it again on the way home (e.g. it is still raining or it is cold) he may do so even if it is still very wet. Otherwise, he must leave it there.

301. What if he has dry weekday clothes?

If a Shabbos garment became wet and he removed it, he may wear it again while still wet if the only alternative is a dry weekday garment. He is not obligated to wear weekday clothes to avoid handling the muktzeh Shabbos clothes.

302. Is a wet towel muktzeh?

No, even if it is very wet. This is because most people have an ample supply of towels and are not tempted to wring it out. The same applies to a dishcloth. Squeezing is nevertheless forbidden.

303. Is a wet rag muktzeh?

No, for the same reason. Squeezing is nevertheless forbidden.

304. Is a wet sponge muktzeh?

Yes, since it is impossible to hold it without squeezing. A dry sponge is a *kli shemelachto l'issur*, but opinions differ whether it is type one or type two.

305. Is a wet tablecloth muktzeh?

A wet tablecloth has the same laws as a wet garment. The same applies to a wet bed-sheet. Therefore, if water spills onto it and it becomes very wet, it is muktzeh.

306. How could one remove such a tablecloth or bed-sheet?

Two people may remove it together. This is an exceptional leniency for moving a wet item that is muktzeh. *Chazal* permitted this since each person will guard the other and remind him not to wring it out.

Note: This leniency does not apply to other types of muktzeh articles.

307. What if a child urinated on his bed-sheet?
The sheet is not muktzeh since there is no temptation to wring it.

308. Are baby-wipes muktzeh?
Yes. It is forbidden to use all types of baby-wipes since their use inevitably involves squeezing. Even if it would be possible to use them without squeezing there is a great temptation to squeeze, and therefore they are comparable to a wet garment.

Fruits and Juices

309. Why is fallen fruit muktzeh?
There are two reasons:
- A special decree was enacted to guard against the temptation to pick fruit on Shabbos.
- Since the fruit was on the tree at the beginning of Shabbos, it was not then available. It is therefore an unprepared item. See Question 458.

310. What if the fruit might have fallen off before Shabbos?
If one is unsure whether the fruit fell off before or on Shabbos, it is still muktzeh.

311. What if it fell off a gentile's tree?
Although the second reason does not apply, the first reason does. Therefore, the fruit is muktzeh. The same applies to fruit that a gentile picked on Shabbos.

312. Which seeped juices are muktzeh?

- Juice that seeped out of grapes is muktzeh whether he is pleased or upset about what happened.
- Juice that seeped out of other fruits is muktzeh if he is pleased about what happened.

313. What if he is indifferent about the juice of other fruits?

This depends on his original intention as follows:

- If he intended to eat the fruit and not squeeze it, the juice is not muktzeh since he will not be tempted to squeeze.
- If he intended to squeeze the fruit, the juice is muktzeh since he will definitely be tempted to squeeze.
- If he was undecided whether to eat or squeeze the fruit, the juice is muktzeh since he might decide to squeeze.

Examples include oranges, grapefruit, watermelon, pomegranates, and strawberries.

314. Why are grapes different?

Grapes are very commonly squeezed for their juice. Even if a person intended to eat his grapes rather than squeeze them, once the juice has seeped out he might change his mind and be tempted to squeeze them. Therefore, the juice is always muktzeh.

315. What if one cuts a juicy fruit?

Juice often drips out of fruit when it is cut, and such juice is subject to the above rules. Therefore, with the exception of grapes it is not muktzeh, and it may be used provided that one intended to eat the fruit and not squeeze it. For example, one may cut up a variety of fruits to make a salad, and the juice that seeps out may be added to the salad. Similarly, after all the salad has been eaten one may drink any remaining juice.

Note: When cutting up fruit on Shabbos, one must avoid the melacha of *tochein* (grinding). This is done by cutting the pieces larger than usual and shortly before the meal.

316. How do the rules apply to lemons?

Although lemons are commonly squeezed for their juice, they are not comparable to grapes but rather to other fruits. The reason is because lemon juice is not drunk on its own but is added to other foods for flavoring. Therefore, juice that seeps out of lemons, whether by itself or when cutting them, is not muktzeh.

Chapter Nine
Muktzeh Machmas Mitzvah

317. What is *muktzeh machmas mitzvah*?
It is an item that is forbidden to use for personal needs since it has been reserved for fulfilling a mitzvah.

318. What are the laws of *muktzeh machmas mitzvah*?
It may not be moved directly even if it is needed for some permitted purpose or one needs to use the place where it is lying. It may only be moved in an indirect or unusual way if necessary. Contrast Question 60.

319. What are examples?
- Succah decorations.
- The *s'chach*.
- The *arba minim*.

320. When do succah decorations become muktzeh?
At sunset on *erev Succos*.

321. Are they muktzeh after Succos?
No, they are only muktzeh until the end of Succos, including *Shemini Atzeres* and *Simchas Torah*. In *Chutz La'aretz* if *Simchas Torah* falls on Friday, they remain muktzeh until *motzai Shabbos*.

322. Are drapes attached to the succah walls muktzeh?

Yes, since they enhance the succah. Therefore, one must be very careful not to touch them with one's hands on Shabbos or Yom Tov since even slight movement of muktzeh is forbidden (see Question 4). It is not forbidden to touch them with one's body when walking around the succah.

323. What if a drape is used in place of a door?

It is not muktzeh, and it may be opened and closed as needed. The same applies to a curtain over a window.

324. What if decorations fell down?

They remain muktzeh and may not be moved directly. If they fall onto the table, one may push them off in an indirect or unusual way.

325. What if fallen decorations contain words of Torah?

Although these are also muktzeh, they must still be treated with respect. Therefore, if they fall onto the table and are in the way, or if they fall onto the floor, they should be picked up with the back of the hands and moved to a suitable place.

326. What if decorations were removed from the succah during *Chol Hamoed*?

One is still forbidden to use them for personal needs, and therefore they remain muktzeh on Shabbos and Yom Yov.

327. When does the *s'chach* become muktzeh?

S'chach is muktzeh all year round since it has no use on Shabbos (*muktzeh machmas gufo*). In addition, the *s'chach* on the succah is *muktzeh machmas mitzvah* during Succos since it has been reserved for a mitzvah.

328. What if some *s'chach* falls down during Succos?

It remains muktzeh. If it falls down onto the table, one may push it off in an indirect or unusual way. If many leaves or twigs fall onto the table and one is repulsed by them, one may remove them by hand, see Question 496. See also Questions 520 and 521.

329. What if some *s'chach* was blown out of position by the wind on Shabbos or Yom Tov?

One may not move it back into place even indirectly such as with a broom since doing so might transgress the *melacha* of *boneh* (building). A Rav should be consulted to determine whether the succah is still kosher. However, one may directly tell a gentile to put the *s'chach* in its proper place.

330. Do all the *arba minim* have the same laws?

No, the laws are as follows:
- The *lulav* and *aravos* are *muktzeh machmas gufo* on any Shabbos since they have no use.
- The *hadassim* on any Shabbos except Succos are not muktzeh since one may smell them. However, if

the owner does not allow anyone to handle or smell them, they are *muktzeh machmas chisaron kis*.

- The *hadassim* on Shabbos during Succos are *muktzeh machmas mitzvah* since they have been designated for a mitzvah, and it is forbidden to smell them. However, if they have not yet been used for the mitzvah of *arba minim* (e.g. the first day of Succos is Shabbos) they are not yet muktzeh and may be smelled (unless the owner objects).
- Regarding the *esrog*, see Question 131.

331. May one smell the *hadassim* on *Simchas Torah*?

Yes, since they are no longer reserved for the mitzvah.

332. Which *b'racha* should be recited?

Baruch Ata Hashem... borei atzei vesamim.

333. Why is the *esrog* not muktzeh on Shabbos during Succos?

Although the *esrog* has been reserved for a mitzvah, this only forbids a person to use it for its primary purpose, namely eating it. Smelling it is a secondary use, and this is not restricted by its mitzvah reservation. Since one may smell the *esrog*, it is not muktzeh unless the owner forbids people to smell it. This is in contrast to *hadassim* which may not be smelled since that is their primary use.

334. Which *b'racha* should be recited when smelling an *esrog*?

Baruch Ata Hashem... hanosein rei'ach tov bapeiros (Who imbues a pleasant fragrance in fruits). However, according to some opinions, this *b'racha* should not be recited during Succos but only before or after Succos. Therefore, it is preferable not to smell the *esrog* during Succos.

335. Is a shofar *muktzeh machmas mitzvah*?

No. On any Shabbos, including when Rosh Hashanah falls on Shabbos, a shofar is a *kli shemelachto l'issur* type two. If the owner does not allow people to blow it during the year, it is *muktzeh machmas chisaron kis*.

Chapter Ten
Nolad

336. What is *nolad*?

Literally meaning 'born', it refers to an item that came into existence on Shabbos. Since it was not ready for use at the beginning of Shabbos, it is muktzeh. There are two types of *nolad*:

- Absolute *nolad* - something that did not exist at all.
- Ordinary *nolad* - something that existed before Shabbos but changed its form on Shabbos.

Absolute *nolad* is muktzeh on both Shabbos and Yom Tov, whereas ordinary *nolad* is muktzeh on Yom Tov but not on Shabbos.

337. What are the rules of *nolad*?

It may not be moved directly even if it is needed for some permitted purpose or one needs to use the place where it is lying. It may only be moved in an indirect or unusual way if necessary. Contrast Question 60.

Absolute Nolad

338. What are examples of absolute *nolad*?
- A newly laid egg.
- Milk from a cow.
- Water produced by air conditioning (see also Question 468).

These are muktzeh both on Shabbos and on Yom Tov.

339. Is a mother's milk *nolad*?
Milk that she expresses on Shabbos and Yom Tov is *nolad* and therefore muktzeh. Nevertheless, she may feed her baby as usual, and she may also express milk to waste to relieve herself from pain. In certain circumstances, she may use an electric pump connected to a Shabbos clock in order to extract milk for the baby. Although such milk is muktzeh, it may be fed to the baby since its life is dependent on the milk. However, the milk should not be handled more than necessary.

340. Is a new-born baby muktzeh?
No! A live human being is never muktzeh.

341. Is rain muktzeh?
No. Rain that falls on Shabbos or Yom Tov is not *nolad* since it existed in the clouds beforehand. However, if it is dirty and unfit for use, it is muktzeh.

342. Is snow muktzeh?

- According to most opinions, snow is like rain and is not muktzeh.
- According to some opinions, snow is muktzeh even if it fell before Shabbos or Yom Tov since it has no use. Nevertheless, one may walk on snow on Shabbos or Yom Tov since it is permitted to move muktzeh with one's body (see Question 438).

Note: According to all opinions, it is forbidden to make snowballs and snowmen on Shabbos or Yom Tov due to the *melacha* of *boneh* (building).

Ordinary Nolad

343. What are examples of ordinary *nolad*?

- Bones of chicken and meat that became separated from the food and are fit for animals.
- Peels and pits of fruits and vegetables that became separated from the food and are fit for animals. See also Question 208.
- A utensil that broke and the pieces are usable for some purpose other than its original use.
- A utensil that was made by a gentile.

If these occurred on Shabbos, the items are ordinary *nolad* and are not muktzeh. However, if they occurred on Yom Tov, the items are muktzeh.

344. What if the bones are not fit for animals?

They are useless and are muktzeh even on Shabbos. The same applies to peels and pits that are not fit for animals.

345. What is an example of a broken utensil that has a new use?

A garment tore badly and is only usable as a rag. If it tore on Shabbos it is not muktzeh, but if it tore on Yom Tov it is muktzeh.

346. What is an example of a utensil made by a gentile?

A gentile took pieces of wood and built an object from them on Shabbos or Yom Tov. On Shabbos the item is not muktzeh, but on Yom Tov it is muktzeh.

347. How do the laws of *nolad* apply to a frozen liquid that melts?

- On Shabbos, it is usually forbidden to directly cause a frozen liquid to change its form by melting (the details are beyond the scope of this *sefer*). If this was done, whether in a forbidden or permitted way, the melted liquid is not muktzeh.
- On Yom Tov, one may melt or defrost a frozen liquid that is needed that day, and the resulting liquid is not muktzeh. For example: frozen soup may be placed in a pot and heated on a flame; one may use margarine for frying. Similarly, it is permitted to cause the reverse change by making ice cubes or ice cream provided it will be ready to eat on the same day.

Chapter Eleven
Bosis

348. What is a *bosis*?

It is a non-muktzeh object that is used as a base for a muktzeh item. Since the non-muktzeh object is serving the muktzeh by supporting it, it too becomes a muktzeh item. For example, an empty drawer is not muktzeh, but if the drawer contains money it becomes a muktzeh *bosis*. Similarly, a table is a *bosis* if muktzeh items were left on it. However, several conditions must be fulfilled for the base to be muktzeh. These will be explained later in the chapter.

349. What if the muktzeh item is serving the non-muktzeh object?

In this case, the non-muktzeh object is not a *bosis*. For example, a calculator was placed on a pile of papers as a paperweight. Although the papers are beneath the muktzeh calculator, they are not muktzeh since the calculator is serving the papers and not vice versa.

350. What if the non-muktzeh object is above the muktzeh item?

- If the muktzeh item is serving the non-muktzeh object, the latter is not a *bosis*. For example, if a spoon was placed on a tool-box, the spoon is not a *bosis*.

- If the non-muktzeh object is serving the muktzeh item but not supporting it, the non-muktzeh object is not a *bosis*. For example, if a cloth was placed over a sewing machine to keep it clean, the cloth is not muktzeh. Although the cloth is serving the machine, it is not supporting it.
- If the non-muktzeh object is supporting the muktzeh item, it is a *bosis*. For example, if a muktzeh garment is suspended from the clips of a hanger, the hanger and clips are muktzeh (see Question 412). Although they are above the muktzeh garment, they are supporting it.

351. What are the laws of a *bosis*?

A *bosis* receives the laws of the muktzeh that it supports. Therefore:
- If the muktzeh item is severely muktzeh (*muktzeh machmas chisaron kis* or *muktzeh machmas gufo*), the *bosis* is severely muktzeh, i.e. it may not be moved directly for any purpose (see Questions 110 and 139).
- If the muktzeh item is a *kli shemelachto l'issur*, the *bosis* receives the same lenient laws, i.e. it may be moved directly if it is needed or if its place is needed (see Question 60).

352. What are examples of these rules?

- If a bag contains money, the bag may not be moved directly since money is *muktzeh machmas gufo*. If its place is needed, it must be moved in an indirect or unusual way.

- If a drawer contains pots and pans, the drawer becomes a *kli shemelachto l'issur*. Therefore, if a pot or pan is needed for some permitted use, one may open the drawer directly. It must be closed in an indirect or unusual manner unless it is in the way. (Compare Question 87.)

353. What if the muktzeh was removed from the *bosis* during Shabbos?

The *bosis* remains muktzeh for the entire Shabbos. Although it is no longer supporting the muktzeh, it nevertheless remains muktzeh since its status is determined at the beginning of Shabbos when it was supporting the muktzeh (see Question 448). There is no difference whether the muktzeh fell off, or it was removed by a child or a gentile. Contrast Question 370.

354. Is there such a thing as a *bosis* to a *bosis*?

Yes. For example:

- Candles were lit in candlesticks that were placed on a tray on a table. Everything is muktzeh, since they are all supporting the burning flame.
- A roll of foil was placed on a stack of plastic chairs. All the chairs are muktzeh since they are all supporting the roll of foil.

355. In the first example, is the tablecloth also muktzeh?

Opinions differ whether the section underneath the tray is muktzeh. The rest of the tablecloth is not muktzeh, and one may sit at the table even if one's hands will move the hanging part of the tablecloth.

356. Under which conditions is a *bosis* muktzeh?

The following points will be discussed:
- Intentional placement.
- Time of placement.
- Placement by the owner.
- Value of the muktzeh.
- Base to muktzeh and non-muktzeh.

Intentional Placement

357. What is meant by intentional placement?

An object is a *bosis* only if the muktzeh item was placed on it deliberately with the intention that it remain there during Shabbos. This excludes the following cases:
- The muktzeh item was placed there deliberately with the intention of removing it before Shabbos, but the person forgot to remove it.
- The muktzeh item fell there accidentally whether before or during Shabbos.

In these situations the object supporting the muktzeh item is not a *bosis*.

358. What if one planned to remove the muktzeh item on Shabbos?

Even if one planned to remove the muktzeh item on Shabbos (e.g. indirectly or via a gentile), the object supporting it is a *bosis* since the muktzeh item was placed there deliberately.

359. What if the muktzeh item was placed there with no specific intention?

- If the muktzeh item is regularly kept there, the supporting object is a *bosis*. For example, a drawer that is used to store muktzeh items is a *bosis* even if the items are put there with no specific intention.
- If the muktzeh item is not kept there regularly and it was placed there on Thursday or earlier in the week, the supporting object is not a *bosis*.
- If the muktzeh item is not kept there regularly and it was placed there on Friday, opinions differ whether the supporting object is a *bosis*. It is preferable to be strict in this situation, especially if the item was put there while tidying the house for Shabbos.

360. What if one intended to place a non-muktzeh item with the muktzeh item but forgot?

An object that is a base to both a muktzeh and a non-muktzeh item is usually not a *bosis* (see Question 394). However, if one placed a muktzeh item on an object deliberately and intended to place there also a non-muktzeh item but subsequently forgot, the object becomes a *bosis*. For example, a woman lit candles on the dining-room table planning to place challos there also. If she forgot to put the challos there until nightfall, the table is a muktzeh *bosis*. See also Question 365.

361. What if a muktzeh item was placed on a non-muktzeh item in the freezer?

There is a type of semi-deliberate placement called chance placement. This refers to a situation where muktzeh was placed above non-muktzeh not for support but simply out of convenience. For example, raw chicken was placed inside a freezer above a block of ice cream because there was no other room for it. Opinions differ whether the non-muktzeh item (the ice cream) became a *bosis*. It is preferable to be strict unless there is a need to use the non-muktzeh item.

362. What are other examples of this situation?

• A person packed a variety of items into a suitcase. When opening the suitcase on Shabbos, he sees that he had placed a muktzeh item on a non-muktzeh item.

• In a drawer full of muktzeh and non-muktzeh items, some muktzeh items were placed above non-muktzeh items due to lack of space.

Opinions differ whether the non-muktzeh items are a *bosis*.

Time of Placement

363. What is meant by time of placement?

An object only becomes a *bosis* if it supports a muktzeh item throughout the entire time from sunset until nightfall. If the muktzeh item was not there for some of the time, the object does not become a *bosis*. For example, the muktzeh item fell off or was removed by a child or a gentile before nightfall.

364. What if a non-muktzeh item was also there for some of the time?

If a person wishes to prevent an object from becoming a *bosis*, he must place on it a non-muktzeh item together with the muktzeh item (see Question 394). Ideally, the non-muktzeh item should be there throughout the entire time from sunset until nightfall. However, even if the non-muktzeh item was there for some of the time, the object does not become a *bosis*.

365. What is an example?

A woman lit candles on the dining room table. If she wishes to prevent the table from becoming a *bosis*, she should ensure that something non-muktzeh such as challos are also on the table from sunset. However, if she forgot to do so, it is still effective to place the challos there until nightfall. In *Eretz Yisroel* the custom is to consider nightfall to be twenty minutes after sunset for this purpose.

366. Should the challos already be there when she lights candles?

This is not necessary. It is sufficient to put them on the table shortly before sunset.

367. What if the non-muktzeh item was removed before nightfall?

The supporting object does not become a *bosis* since the non-muktzeh item was there for some of the time. For example, instead of challos she placed her siddur on the table before sunset. Shortly after sunset, she picked up her siddur in order to *daven Kabbalas Shabbos*. The table does not become a *bosis*. Nevertheless, she should replace the siddur with some other non-muktzeh item so that something non-muktzeh is there the entire time until nightfall. See Question 364.

368. Are the laws affected by accepting Shabbos early?

No. Even if the family accepts Shabbos early, the laws of *bosis* are determined by the object's status from sunset until nightfall.

369. Can an object become a *bosis* during Shabbos?

If a muktzeh item was deliberately placed on an object (e.g. by a child or gentile) during Shabbos, opinions differ whether the object becomes a *bosis*. It is preferable to consider the object as a *bosis*.

370. Does this *bosis* have the same laws as a regular *bosis*?

No. For convenience, we shall refer to a regular *bosis* as a 'permanent *bosis*' and a *bosis* made on Shabbos as a 'temporary *bosis*'. A 'permanent *bosis*' remains muktzeh throughout Shabbos even if the muktzeh item was removed during Shabbos, i.e. its status is permanent (see Question 353). In contrast, a 'temporary *bosis*' is muktzeh only while the muktzeh is on it. Since it was not a *bosis* at the beginning of Shabbos, its status is changeable. Therefore, if the muktzeh is subsequently removed, the base returns to its previous status and is no longer muktzeh.

371. How could one remove the muktzeh item from a 'temporary *bosis*'?

The item could be removed in an unusual way, such as by knocking it off with one's elbow, see Question 438. Opinions differ whether one may tilt the base for the muktzeh item to fall.

372. What is an example?

A child walked into the dining-room during Shabbos holding a raw potato, and the parent told him to place it on a chair. According to some opinions, the chair has become a 'temporary *bosis*' and may not be moved. If the chair is needed later one may knock off the potato, and the chair is no longer muktzeh.

373. What if a non-muktzeh item is placed on a *bosis* during Shabbos?

- A 'permanent *bosis*' is not affected by such placement since its status cannot be changed.
- A 'temporary *bosis*' would cease to be muktzeh since its status is changeable. (The non-muktzeh item must be more important than the muktzeh item, see Question 396.) In the example above, if a spoon were placed on the chair, the chair would no longer be muktzeh and could be moved if it is in the way.

374. Can an object become a 'temporary *bosis*' in any other way?

Yes, this can happen as follows: at the beginning of Shabbos an object was a base to a muktzeh item and a non-muktzeh item, and therefore it was not a *bosis*. During Shabbos, the non-muktzeh item was removed, leaving only the muktzeh item on the base. According to some opinions, the base has become a 'temporary *bosis*'. It is preferable to be strict in this matter.

375. What could be done in this situation?

A non-muktzeh item could be placed on the 'temporary *bosis*', thereby removing its status of muktzeh. For example, challos were on the dining room table when Shabbos candles were lit there. After the evening meal, the table was cleared leaving only the Shabbos candles on it. According to some opinions, the table is a 'temporary *bosis*' and may not be moved. If a non-muktzeh item is then placed on the table, the table is no longer muktzeh. See also Question 396.

376. Would the same apply to a drawer?

Yes. If a drawer contains a variety of items, some muktzeh and one that is not, it is often not a *bosis* (see Questions 394 and 395). If the drawer is opened and the non-muktzeh item is removed, the drawer becomes a 'temporary *bosis*' according to some opinions and may only be closed in an indirect or unusual way. If one places an important non-muktzeh object in the drawer, the drawer may be closed normally (see Question 396). The same could apply to a suitcase.

Placement by the Owner

377. What does placement by the owner mean?

An object only becomes a *bosis* if its owner places the muktzeh item on it or allows the muktzeh item to be there.

378. Does it matter who owns the muktzeh item?

No, this is irrelevant.

379. What is an example?

A Shabbos guest placed his muktzeh items on a chair in the room that he was given. If the host objects to the chair being used that way, it is not a *bosis*. However, if the host told his guest to feel at home and use the room as he wishes, the chair becomes a *bosis*.

380. Could a wife make her husband's belongings a *bosis*?

If she uses that object freely with her husband's knowledge, it can become a *bosis*. The same applies to children who have permission to use various objects as if they owned them.

381. Does this apply to children to below bar/bas mitzvah?

No. Children below bar/bas mitzvah cannot cause an object to become a *bosis* since their intentions are not sufficiently mature. However, if the child was obeying the instructions of his parent, his placement of a muktzeh item would make a *bosis*. See Question 372.

382. What if the object is shared by two or more people?

If one of the partners places a muktzeh item on a shared object, it becomes a *bosis* since each partner has the right to use the object as he wishes. For example, several yeshiva boys who share the use of a table in their dormitory room.

383. Does the same apply to an object shared by the public?

No. Although each individual has the right to use the object, nevertheless he does not have the power to forbid its use to the public by making it a *bosis*. For example, if a person placed a muktzeh item on a *shtender* in shul, the *shtender* is not a *bosis*.

Value of the Muktzeh

384. Why is the value of the muktzeh relevant?

If the muktzeh item is of little or no value, the object on which it is placed does not usually become a *bosis*. In this situation, the object is not considered as serving the muktzeh item, and it retains its own non-muktzeh status. For example: a scrap of paper or a few pennies in a drawer or pocket, bones or shells on a plate.

385. What is considered significant value?

The muktzeh item has significant value if the owner would bother to bend down and pick it off the floor.

386. When is there an exception?

An exception is when the object has been designated to hold insignificant muktzeh items. For example: a garbage bin containing waste, a purse containing a few pennies. These are a *bosis*.

387. Is the cover of a garbage bin muktzeh?

No. The cover does not serve the garbage or the bin, rather it serves people so that they will not see or smell the garbage. Therefore, it may be opened and closed as usual when discarding waste items. There is no difference whether the cover is attached to the bin or is a separate piece.

388. May one open the top of the bag that contains garbage?

Yes. Although the main part of the bag that contains garbage is a *bosis*, the clean top part is not muktzeh and may be opened for further use. Compare Question 355.

389. Is there any way to move the garbage bin?

- If it contained garbage at the beginning of Shabbos, it is a *bosis* and may only be moved in an unusual way, e.g. with one's foot.
- If it is empty, it is a *kli shemelachto l'issur* (see Question 53). It may be moved by hand in order to throw garbage in.
- If it contains garbage but was empty at the beginning of Shabbos, opinions differ whether it is a *bosis* (see Question 369). It is preferable to be strict and only move it in an unusual way.

390. What if the garbage bin is inside a drawer?

If there is garbage in the bin, the drawer is also a *bosis* and may only be opened and closed in an unusual way. A practical suggestion is to leave a spare garbage bag in the drawer next to the bin. The drawer then supports both the muktzeh garbage and the non-muktzeh bag, and it is therefore not a *bosis*.

391. What if the garbage bin is attached to a cabinet door?

Opinions differ whether the door is a *bosis* since the door serves both the garbage and the room. One should preferably hang a spare bag on the door in order to guarantee that the door is not a *bosis*.

392. May one throw out a full garbage bag?

If one is repulsed by the sight or the bad smell of the garbage, one may remove it, see Question 490. It may be taken outside if there is an *eiruv*. If one is not repulsed, it may not be moved since it is a *bosis*.

393. Does a dustpan become a *bosis* when sweeping the floor?

No. Although the dustpan is designated to hold garbage, it does not become a *bosis* since the garbage is on it for only a very short time. When a muktzeh item is placed on an object with the intention of removing it soon after, the object does not become a *bosis*. Similarly, if one peels fruit or shells eggs over a dish with the intention to throw the peels or shells into the garbage, the dish does not become a *bosis*.

Base to Muktzeh and Non-muktzeh

394. What is a base to muktzeh and non-muktzeh?

It is a non-muktzeh object that is supporting both muktzeh and non-muktzeh items. For example: a drawer, bag, or suitcase containing muktzeh and non-muktzeh items; a table on which Shabbos candles and challos were placed.

395. Is such a base considered a muktzeh *bosis*?

Such a base is considered to be primarily serving the most important item, and its status is determined accordingly. If the most important item is muktzeh the base becomes a *bosis*, but if the most important item is not muktzeh the base does not become a *bosis*.

396. How is the most important item determined?

- If there is a non-muktzeh item that is needed on Shabbos, that item is deemed the most important. This applies even if its monetary value is less than the muktzeh item. For example, challos are considered more important than silver candlesticks.
- If there is no non-muktzeh item that is needed on Shabbos, the most important item is the one that is the most expensive. The base will have the same status as that item whether it is muktzeh or non-muktzeh.

397. What if the needed non-muktzeh item was not needed at the beginning of Shabbos?

In that case, the non-muktzeh item is not automatically considered the most important item. Rather, the most expensive item is the most important. For example, a drawer contained a large amount of money and a packet of tissues. The tissues were not needed at the beginning of Shabbos since there were other tissues in the house. If the other tissues were used up during Shabbos and those in the drawer were then needed, the drawer is nevertheless a *bosis* to the money and may only be opened in an unusual way.

398. How do these rules apply to a candlestick tray?

Some people wish to prevent the candlestick tray from becoming a *bosis* in order to be able to remove it from the table after the candles have burned out. They do this by placing on the tray next to the candlesticks a needed non-muktzeh item such as a ring, a *zemiros* book, or some food. This procedure is effective only if the tray is often used for other purposes such as serving food. However, if the tray is used exclusively for holding the candlesticks, it is a *bosis* even if one places a needed non-muktzeh item on it. The reason is because such a tray is primarily serving the candlesticks and not the non-muktzeh item.

399. What if a muktzeh item is hanging on a door?

The door does not become a *bosis* since it primarily serves the room and not the muktzeh item hanging on it. For example: a bag with money hanging on a bedroom door, flour inside the door of a refrigerator or freezer. The door may be opened and closed as usual. See Question 94.

Tilting

400. What is meant by tilting?

In many situations, a base to a muktzeh item does not become a *bosis*. Nevertheless, movement of the base is usually restricted since this will indirectly cause the muktzeh item to move. Therefore, before one moves the base he is required to tilt it so that the muktzeh item will fall off.

401. What is an example?

A purse was unintentionally left on a chair. Although the chair is not a *bosis* (see Question 357), it may not be moved unless one first tilts the purse off.

402. When is tilting not required?

Tilting is not required in the following cases:
- It is physically impossible.
- The surrounding area is needed.
- Tilting could cause damage to surrounding items.
- Tilting could cause damage to the muktzeh item.

403. When is tilting physically impossible?

For example:
- A drawer contains muktzeh and non-muktzeh items. One may open the drawer to take a needed non-muktzeh item since tilting the drawer to remove the muktzeh items is impossible.
- The door of a refrigerator holds muktzeh items. One may open the door to take food since it impossible to tilt the door. See also Question 399.

404. When is the surrounding area needed?

For example, a suitcase contains muktzeh and non-muktzeh items. If one needs a non-muktzeh item from the suitcase, one should remove it without moving the suitcase or any muktzeh items. If this is not possible, one should empty out all the contents of the suitcase onto the floor. If that area must be kept clear for people to walk through, he may carry the suitcase to a different place and spill out the items there.

405. When could tilting cause damage to surrounding items?

For example, a child placed a rock on a chair in the garden. If the chair is needed one should tilt off the rock onto the ground. If there are surrounding flowers that will be damaged by the falling rock, one may carry the chair with the rock to a suitable place where tilting can be done safely.

406. When could tilting cause damage to the muktzeh item?

For example, a camera was unintentionally left on a pillow that is needed for sleeping. If there is a stone floor, one is not required to tilt the pillow and risk damage to the camera. One may carry the pillow and camera to a carpeted room and do the tilting there. If there are no carpets, one should bring a soft garment or similar item and tilt the camera onto it. See also Question 475.

Chapter Twelve
Pockets and Drawers

Pockets

407. How do the laws of *bosis* apply to pockets?

It is not rare for a muktzeh item, such as money, to be accidentally left in a pocket of a Shabbos garment that was worn on a weekday. The garment is not a *bosis* since the wearer probably wanted to remove the muktzeh item before Shabbos but forgot to do so (see Question 357). Nevertheless, if one wishes to move the garment, he should first shake the muktzeh item from the pocket (see Question 400).

408. What if the item does not fall out?

One should try to remove it by manipulating the material of the pocket or by scooping it out with a spoon or similar item.

409. What if he is unsuccessful in removing it?

He may move the garment with the muktzeh item in the pocket. However, it is forbidden to wear the garment due to a concern that he might forget about the item and walk outside, thereby transgressing the *melacha* of *hotza'ah* (carrying).

410. When would a pocket become a *bosis*?

When the muktzeh item was put there intentionally, and one was content before Shabbos to leave it there during Shabbos. This could occur when he needed unexpectedly to wear a weekday garment on Shabbos, e.g. if his Shabbos garment become soiled or very wet.

411. Is the entire garment a *bosis*?

This depends on the type of pocket, as follows:
- A patch pocket: this is a flat piece of material sewn onto the garment on three sides, e.g. a shirt pocket.
- An independent pocket: this resembles a small cloth bag attached around its opening, and usually hangs on the inside of the garment, e.g. an inside pocket in a jacket.

412. What are the laws of a patch pocket?

If a muktzeh item was intentionally left in a patch pocket, the entire garment is a *bosis* and may not be worn or moved even if the muktzeh item is removed. The reason is because the garment itself forms the inner wall of the pocket, and the muktzeh item is lying on the garment.

413. What if the garment is hanging between others?

If such a garment is hanging in a closet between others, one must take care not to move it directly along the rod when removing a Shabbos garment. One must move it only indirectly by pushing it with another garment, see Question 427.

414. What are the laws of an independent pocket?

If a muktzeh item was intentionally left in an independent pocket, the pocket is a *bosis* but the rest of the garment is not muktzeh. The reason is because the muktzeh item is not supported by the primary part of the garment but only by the secondary part, i.e. the pocket. Therefore, one should shake the garment in order to remove the muktzeh item.

415. What if the item does not fall out?

One may not manipulate the material of the pocket since the pocket is muktzeh. He may try to remove it by scooping it out with a spoon or similar item. If he succeeds in removing it he may wear the garment, but he must be very careful not to put his hand into the pocket since the pocket remains muktzeh for the entire Shabbos. If he is unsuccessful in removing it, he may not wear the garment (see Question 409).

416. What if one discovers a muktzeh item in a garment that he is wearing?

If it is a Shabbos garment, it is not muktzeh (see Question 407). Nevertheless, he should shake out the muktzeh item since one may not wear a garment with a muktzeh item in the pocket (see Question 409). If necessary, he should take off the garment in order to shake it.

417. What if he is embarrassed to do this?

If he is in public and is embarrassed to shake out the muktzeh item or to take off the garment, he may walk to a discreet place in order to remove the muktzeh item. This is only permitted outdoors where there is an *eiruv* or indoors. If this occurred outdoors where there is no *eiruv*, the laws are complex and beyond the scope of this *sefer*.

Drawers

418. How do the laws of *bosis* apply to drawers?

This depends on whether the drawer is removable or not, as follows:

- A removable drawer is considered to be a separate object that is supported by a piece of furniture. This is the case for most tables, desks, dressers, and kitchen cabinets.

- A non-removable drawer is comparable to an independent pocket and has parallel laws. This is the case for many filing cabinets.

419. What if the drawer is not readily removable?

Some drawers are held in place with plastic catches that must be opened to remove the drawer. Since this is simple to do and requires no tools, the drawer is considered removable. If tools are needed to detach the drawer, it is considered non-removable.

420. What are the laws of a removable drawer?

For the sake of clarity, we will first discuss a desk with one removable drawer.

- If there is a muktzeh item in the drawer and nothing on the desk, both the drawer and the desk are a *bosis* and may not be moved.
- If there is a muktzeh item in the drawer and a more important non-muktzeh item on the desk, the drawer is a *bosis* and may not be moved. However, the desk is not a *bosis* and may be moved since it is supporting both the muktzeh and non-muktzeh items.
- If there is no muktzeh item in the drawer, it may be moved. This applies even when there is a muktzeh item on the desk.

421. What is the law of the desk in the last case?

If there is a muktzeh item on the desk, opinions differ whether the desk is considered a base only to the muktzeh item on it or also to the drawer. It is preferable not to move the desk.

422. What is the general rule for a removable drawer?

The status of a removable drawer is not affected by the desk, but the status of the desk is affected by the drawer. Therefore, one may always open and close the drawer if it does not contain anything muktzeh.

423. How do the laws apply to a dresser with several removable drawers?

Each drawer is independent of the other. A drawer that contains muktzeh items must not be moved; a drawer that does not contain anything muktzeh may be opened and closed.

424. What are the laws of a non-removable drawer?

The desk and the drawer are independent of each other. Therefore, the desk may be moved unless there is a muktzeh item on it, and the drawer may be moved unless there is a muktzeh item inside it. A muktzeh item on one does not affect the other. Similarly, if there are several such drawers, they are all independent of each other.

Chapter Thirteen
Different Types of Movement

425. What is meant by different types of movement?

In certain circumstances, a muktzeh item may be moved in different ways, as follows:
- Indirect movement. This refers to moving a muktzeh item via a non-muktzeh item, e.g. carrying shells on a plate.
- Body movement. This refers to moving a muktzeh item with a part of one's body other than the hands, e.g. kicking.

Indirect Movement

426. Is indirect movement permitted for all types of muktzeh items?

Yes. All four types of muktzeh items may be moved indirectly, see Question 7.

427. When is indirect movement permitted?

Generally, this is permitted in two cases:
1. In order to use the place where the muktzeh item is lying. This includes the situation where a muktzeh item is blocking one's way.
2. In honor of Shabbos.

Note: If the muktzeh item is a *kli shemelachto l'issur*, regular movement is permitted in the first case, see Question 60.

428. What are examples of the first case?
- Eggs were shelled over a plate on the counter. If the space on the counter is needed, one may carry the plate to the garbage bin and empty out the shells.
- Leftover food, bones, etc. may be scraped off a plate into the garbage using a knife.
- If muktzeh toys are scattered on the floor and one is afraid of tripping over them, one may push them into a corner with a broom.
- If a calculator was left on a shelf and one needs a *sefer* behind it, one may move it aside with a spoon.

429. What is an example of the second case?
In honor of Shabbos, one may sweep garbage off the floor with a broom into a dustpan and empty it into the bin.

430. What if moving a non-muktzeh item causes a muktzeh item to move?
This is also considered a permitted form of indirect movement. For example:
- One may take ice cream from a freezer even if this causes surrounding muktzeh foods to move.
- One may take tissues from a drawer even if this causes surrounding muktzeh items to move.

Care should be taken not to inadvertently move a muktzeh item directly.

431. May one move a muktzeh item indirectly to protect it?

No. For example:

- A muktzeh item was found on the floor in the house. One may not push it under a bed or couch with a broom to prevent damage or loss. See also Question 441.
- A cellphone was forgotten outside on a chair. One may not carry the chair inside to protect the cellphone from the rain or burglars. Rather, one may cover the cellphone and leave it outside.

432. May one cover a muktzeh item for protection if it will move slightly?

No, this is a forbidden form of indirect movement.

433. Is indirect movement permitted when it is the usual way?

Yes. For example, one may sweep the floor even though this is the usual way to move dirt and garbage.

434. May one pick up a child who is holding a muktzeh item?

This is usually forbidden. The child is not considered to be an intermediary object, rather the adult is considered to be moving the muktzeh directly together with the child.

435. May one shake the child's arm?

This is indirect movement of the item and is usually permitted. However, it is forbidden in the following two cases:
- One is doing so due to fear that the child might break or lose the item, see Question 431.
- The child is holding money or a valuable item, see next question.

436. When may one pick up the child?

If the child refuses to release an inexpensive item and will become very upset if he is not held, one may pick him up. *Chazal* were lenient in this case in order to prevent the child from becoming sick. However, if the child is holding money or a valuable item, one may not pick up the child even in this situation. The reason is that the child might release the item, and the adult might inadvertently pick it up. Similarly, one may not shake his arm.

437. May one walk with the child and hold his other hand?

- If the child is holding a muktzeh item of little value, this is permitted.
- If the child is holding money or a valuable muktzeh item, opinions differ whether this is permitted. One should be strict unless there is an urgent need, e.g. the child might run away.

Body Movement

438. What is meant by body movement?

This means moving a muktzeh item with a part of one's body other than the hands. For example: using one's foot, knee, elbow, shoulder, or teeth.

439. Is body movement permitted for all types of muktzeh items?

Yes.

440. When is body movement permitted?

Unlike indirect movement, body movement is permitted even for the protection of the muktzeh item (contrast Question 431). Body movement is certainly permitted when indirect movement is permitted, i.e. in order to use the place of the muktzeh item or in honor of Shabbos. See Questions 428 and 429.

441. What are examples of protection?

- A muktzeh item was found on the floor in the house. One may kick it under a bed or couch to prevent damage or loss.
- When taking a challah out of the freezer, a raw chicken starts to fall out. One may push it back in with one's elbow.

442. Is body movement permitted when it is the usual way?

Unlike indirect movement, body movement is forbidden when it is the usual way (contrast Question 433). For example, if one's watch stopped while he was wearing it, he should remove it immediately. If possible, he should remove it in an unusual way such as with his teeth. He may not continue to wear it and claim that he is only moving it with his wrist since this is the usual way. See also Questions 104 and 105. Similarly, one may not move a portable heater with his foot if he usually does this on weekdays.

443. May one move a muktzeh item with the back of the hand?

Use of one's hand in any way does not qualify as body movement. Nevertheless, using the back of the hand is a slight deviation from normal, and it is subject to the same laws as indirect movement. Therefore, it is permitted to move it in order to use the place of the muktzeh item or in honor of Shabbos but not to protect the item (see Question 427). The same laws apply to use of one's forearm.

444. May one move a muktzeh item by blowing at it?

Yes, this is considered a form of body movement. For example, if an ant is crawling on a table or counter, one may blow it off.

445. May one sit on a muktzeh item?

Yes. Even if this causes the item to move, it is called body movement. Nevertheless, if the item will move, it is preferable to refrain since one might inadvertently move the item with his hands. Contrast Question 149.

Asking a Gentile

446. May one ask a gentile to move a muktzeh item?

This is permitted in the following cases:
1. To move a *kli shemelachto l'issur* to protect it from damage or loss, see Question 76.
2. To move any type of muktzeh because one needs to use the item or its place.
3. To move any type of item for the sake of a slightly sick person, for the sake of a mitzvah, or to avoid a substantial loss.

Note: The laws of asking a gentile to act on Shabbos on one's behalf are complex, whether one asks on Shabbos or a weekday. A Rav should be consulted whenever necessary.

447. What are examples of the third case?

- A person with a slight headache is disturbed by the constant chirping of his pet bird. He may ask a gentile to take it out of the room.
- A deceased person may be removed from a shul by a gentile so that *cohanim* may enter.
- Valuable muktzeh items may be brought indoors by a gentile for fear of damage by rain.

Chapter Fourteen
Fixed Status

448. What is meant by fixed status?

As explained in Question 1, an item may only be moved on Shabbos if it was prepared for use beforehand. There is a rule of 'fixed status', which means that an item that was not ready for use before Shabbos remains muktzeh throughout Shabbos even if it becomes ready during Shabbos. However, the rule is subject to several conditions that will be explained in this chapter. In contrast, an item that was ready before Shabbos and was not muktzeh could become muktzeh during Shabbos if it ceases to be usable, e.g. it breaks.

449. What is an example of the 'fixed status' rule?

One general example is a *bosis*. An object that was supporting a muktzeh item at the beginning of Shabbos remains muktzeh throughout Shabbos even if the muktzeh item was later removed. See Question 353.

450. What are the conditions for this rule?

1. The item was not ready throughout the period called *bein hashemashos*, i.e. from sunset until nightfall.
2. The item was not ready due to human involvement.
3. It is unknown whether the item will be ready on Shabbos.

451. What does the first condition mean?

The rule of 'fixed status' only applies if the item was muktzeh throughout the entire period of *bein hashemashos*. If the item was not muktzeh for even a very short time during this period, its status is not permanently fixed. Therefore if it becomes usable later, it ceases to be muktzeh.

452. What is an example?

See Question 364.

453. What if one accepts Shabbos early?

The rule is the same, i.e. the critical time is *bein hashemashos* even if one accepts Shabbos early.

454. What does the second condition mean?

The rule of 'fixed status' only applies when a person caused the item to be unprepared for use during Shabbos. However, if this state was due to other reasons, the item would cease to be muktzeh if it became usable.

455. What are examples?

- Fruit that was hung in a succah for decoration remains muktzeh even if it fell down on Shabbos since a person caused it to be muktzeh, see Question 324.
- Raw fruit that is totally inedible before Shabbos is muktzeh. If it ripens on Shabbos, it ceases to be muktzeh since its state of unreadiness was due to natural causes, see Question 169.

456. What if a *kli shemelachto l'issur* breaks on Shabbos?

The rule of 'fixed status' applies since its state of muktzeh was due to human action. Therefore if it breaks and is now only suitable for a permitted use, it remains a *kli shemelachto l'issur* for that Shabbos. For example, a battery operated toy is a *kli shemelachto l'issur* (type one) since it can be used with or without batteries. If it breaks on Shabbos and can no longer work with batteries, it becomes a simple toy. Nevertheless, it remains a *kli shemelachto l'issur* for that Shabbos and only becomes non-muktzeh on the following Shabbos.

457. What if a *muktzeh machmas chisaron kis* breaks on Shabbos?

The rule of 'fixed status' applies since its state of muktzeh was due to human action. For example, a garment that one bought and decided to return is *muktzeh machmas chisaron kis* (see Question 135). If it became torn or soiled on Shabbos and he decided to keep it, it remains muktzeh for that Shabbos.

458. How does this condition apply to fallen fruit?

As explained in Question 309, fruit that fell off a tree on Shabbos is muktzeh since it was not prepared beforehand. Although this appears to be due to a natural cause, it is considered as due to human action since he could have picked it before Shabbos and decided not to do so.

459. What if a hot water tank cooled down during Shabbos?

One may not open the hot water faucet on Shabbos if the temperature of the water is above *yad soledes bo* (43°C/110°F). This is because cold water will enter the tank and will cook on contact with the hot water (see Guidelines to Bishul, Question 64). If the water cooled down on Shabbos to below *yad soledes bo*, one may open the faucet and use the warm water. Although the faucet was muktzeh at the beginning of Shabbos, the rule of 'fixed status' does not apply since his inability to open the faucet was due to *halachic* reasons.

Note: This ruling only applies if the water will not be heated later on Shabbos, e.g. by a boiler set on a timer or by solar panels.

460. What does the third condition mean?

The rule of 'fixed status' only applies if one does not know whether the cause of being muktzeh will continue or stop during Shabbos. If steps have been taken to ensure that the cause of being muktzeh will stop, the item is considered prepared and is not muktzeh.

461. What are examples?

- Grapes were placed outside to dry and turn into raisins. If they were not ready at the beginning of Shabbos, they remain muktzeh throughout Shabbos since one cannot know in advance when they will be ready.

- Raw food was placed on a blech close to Shabbos. Although it is still inedible, it is not muktzeh since it will certainly become fit to eat in due course.

462. How does this rule apply to wet laundry?

As explained in Question 293, a very wet garment is usually muktzeh since one might be tempted to wring it out. Clothes that were spun in a washing machine are not muktzeh since one cannot easily squeeze water from them. If such clothes were hung to dry before Shabbos, one may wear them when they are dry. However, clothes that were very wet at the beginning of Shabbos might remain muktzeh throughout Shabbos depending on the drying conditions.

463. When would the clothes remain muktzeh?

According to most opinions, the rules are as follows:
- If they were hung on an outdoor line in variable weather, they remain muktzeh even when dry.
- If they were hung on an outdoor line in hot weather, they are not muktzeh when dry.
- If they were hung on an indoor line in a warm room or draped over hot radiators, they are not muktzeh when dry.

464. What if wet laundry was put into a dryer shortly before Shabbos?

One should not have a dryer operating on Shabbos since this is degrading to the *kedusha* of Shabbos. If this occurred inadvertently, the clothes are not muktzeh when dry since it was planned to happen.

Note: One may not open the door if this will cause any electrical change, e.g. a light will go off. See also Question 89.

465. Are there other examples of 'fixed status'?

There is a Rabbinic decree against using a tree on Shabbos, which includes placing an item on it or removing an item from it, see Question 148. Therefore if a ball became lodged in a tree before Shabbos and one decided to leave it there, it is muktzeh. Even if it subsequently falls out, it remains muktzeh since all three conditions of 'fixed status' apply (see Question 450).

Chapter Fifteen
Nullifying an Item's Usage

466. What is meant by nullifying an item's usage?
On Shabbos, it is usually forbidden to do something to a non-muktzeh object that will make it unusable since it is considered as though one broke it.

467. What is an example?
If an oil lamp is dripping, one may not place a bowl beneath it to catch the oil. Since the oil is muktzeh, a bowl that catches the drips may not be moved, and therefore the bowl has been made unusable for other purposes. Similarly, one may not put a bowl or plate under a dripping wax candle.

468. Does the same apply to the drainage pipe of an air conditioner?
Yes. Since the water produced by an air conditioner is muktzeh (see Question 338), one may not put a container under the drainage pipe to collect the drips unless it has been set aside for this purpose, see Question 479.

469. May one use an empty pot to catch such drips?

No. An empty pot is a *kli shemelachto l'issur* (see Question 39) and may be moved if it is needed for some purpose (see Question 60). However, it may not be used to catch drips since it would then become totally unusable.

470. May one place a container under a drip before Shabbos?

Yes. Although the item will become unusable on Shabbos, it is permitted to put it in the appropriate place before Shabbos.

471. Is there a permitted way to do this on Shabbos?

Yes, by placing a non-muktzeh item in the container before putting it under the drip. In this situation, one would be allowed to move the container since it is serving both the non-muktzeh item and the muktzeh drips (see Question 394). Even if one does not intend to move the container, its use has not been nullified since one is permitted to move it.

472. May one put a *kli shemelachto l'issur* into an empty drawer?

If one moved a *kli shemelachto l'issur* for a permitted reason (see Question 60), he may put it into an empty drawer. Although the drawer becomes a *bosis* according to some opinions (see Question 369), it too becomes a *kli shemelachto l'issur* and may be opened and closed under certain circumstances (see Question 351). Therefore, the drawer's use has not been totally nullified.

473. Are there other types of examples?

- A muktzeh item may not be maneuvered into an empty drawer since it would then be forbidden to open or close the drawer. This nullifies the use of the drawer. For example, if a camera was left on a chair, one may not tilt the camera into an empty drawer. If there is a more important non-muktzeh item in the drawer, one may tilt the camera in (see previous question).
- One may not use a garment to wipe a dirty spill in a way that would make it unwearable.

474. When is nullification of an object's use permitted on Shabbos?

In the following situations:
1. It is possible to reinstate the object's use immediately.
2. The object has been designated for this purpose. See Question 479.
3. The object is disposable. See Question 482.

475. What does the first situation mean?

If the muktzeh item could be tilted off the non-muktzeh object immediately, the object's use has not been nullified. For example, if a camera was left on a chair, one may tilt it onto a pillow on the floor. The pillow is not considered to be unusable since one could immediately tilt the camera from it onto the floor.

476. What if one will definitely not tilt it off?

- If his intention is obvious to everyone, it is forbidden to nullify the item's use. For example, one may not put a container under an air conditioner's dripping pipe in a carpeted room. He clearly is not prepared to spill out the water and damage the carpet. See Question 471 for a solution.
- If his intention is not obvious, it is permitted to nullify the item's use. For example, the air conditioner drips onto a stone floor. The same applies to the camera on the pillow in the previous question.

477. What if he intends to tilt it off later?

It is usually forbidden to nullify the use of an object even temporarily. For example, if a lit candle is about to fall onto a fireproof surface such as a marble counter, one may not place a utensil under it in order to catch it. Even if he intends to tilt out the candle after it stops burning, nevertheless the utensil is unusable as long as the candle burns.

478. When would it be permitted?

Temporary nullification is permitted in order to avoid a significant loss. For example, if the lit candle would fall onto an expensive tablecloth and burn a hole in it. However, this leniency does not apply to permanent nullification. For example, if a wax candle was dripping onto the tablecloth, one may not place a utensil under it since the wax cannot be shaken off the utensil. See also Question 471.

Chapter Fifteen - Nullifying an Item's Usage

479. What are examples of the second situation?

- A rag may be used to wipe a dirty spill. This is not considered as nullifying the use of the rag since this is precisely what it was designated for. Contrast Question 473.
- Garbage may be placed inside an empty garbage bin since the bin was intended for this usage.

480. May one place garbage on a plate?

As explained in Question 384, a plate does not become a *bosis* when garbage such as bones or shells are placed on it. Furthermore, its usage is not nullified by doing this since one could tilt out the garbage immediately, see Question 475. However, if it is totally impractical to tilt it out, one may not place the garbage on the plate. For example, when the plate is on a tablecloth and the spilt garbage would stain the cloth.

481. What could one do in the last case?

- Put a non-muktzeh item such as a spoon on the plate before placing the garbage on it, see Question 471.
- Use a disposable plate, see next question.

482. What are examples of the third situation?
- A paper napkin may be used to wipe a dirty spill.
- Garbage may be put into a plastic bag.
- Garbage may be put onto a disposable plate.

Since these items are discarded after use, this is not considered as nullifying any possible future use.

483. May one indirectly cause nullification?

Yes. For example, if a drawer contains muktzeh items and a needed non-muktzeh item, one may open the drawer and remove the non-muktzeh item (see Question 394) although this causes the drawer to become unusable according to some opinions (see Question 374).

Chapter Sixteen
Exceptional Circumstances

484. What are exceptional circumstances?
It is sometimes permitted to move a muktzeh item directly in the following situations:
- To prevent injury.
- To remove something repulsive (known as *graf*).
- When already holding it.
- When cleaning oneself or an object.
- For the sake of human dignity.

Preventing Injury

485. What are the rules for preventing injury?
When a muktzeh item might cause harm to someone, it may be moved as follows:
- If injury is very likely to occur to the public, the item may be moved in the regular way.
- If injury is very likely to occur to an individual, the item should preferably be moved in an indirect or unusual way. If this is not possible, it may be moved in the regular way.
- If injury is possible but not highly likely, the item must be moved in an indirect or unusual way.

486. Which items are very likely to cause injury?

- Sharp items. E.g. broken glass, pins and needles, thorns, razor edged tools.
- Extremely hot items. E.g. red-hot metal, burning coal.
- Dangerous chemicals. E.g. acid.

487. Which items are not highly likely to cause injury?

Examples include a rock or matches. Although these might cause harm, the likelihood is not so high. Therefore, they may only be moved in an indirect or unusual way.

488. How many people are considered to be the public?

Three or more people even in a private area are considered to be the public for these laws. Furthermore, in a place where there is a baby or very young child crawling or walking around, the lenient laws of the public apply.

489. May one remove medicines from children's reach?

Although most medicines are muktzeh (see Question 174), they may be moved if children could take hold of them, see Question 180.

Chapter Sixteen - Exceptional Circumstances

Repulsive Items

490. What are the rules for repulsive items?
If a repulsive muktzeh item is in a place that one is using on Shabbos, one may remove it in the regular way.

491. Is it preferable to ask a gentile to move it?
According to most opinions, this is not necessary. Similarly, one is not required to move it in an indirect or unusual way.

492. What are examples?
A dirty diaper, foul smelling garbage, dead roaches and mice.

493. What if a full garbage bin is unsightly but not foul smelling?
- If the bin is inside a cabinet or has a cover, it is not considered repulsive.
- If it is in the room without a cover, it might be considered repulsive to some people.

494. Is repulsiveness objective or subjective?
It is subjective. People have different levels of sensitivity, and one who is easily repulsed may be more lenient.

495. May one who is not repulsed move the item for someone who is?

Yes.

496. Could peels and shells on the table be considered repulsive?

It is considered repulsive if one would feel embarrassed about its presence were guests to arrive and see it.

497. Could a dirty pot be considered repulsive?

Yes. If someone in the house is repulsed by it, one may remove it directly.

498. To which areas of the house does the exemption apply?

It applies only to areas used during Shabbos. One may not move a repulsive item directly from an unused place, e.g. storage basement, attic, garage. The exemption would apply to a porch, yard, or garden if these areas will be used on that Shabbos.

499. May one decide to use an area in order to remove the item?

If a repulsive item is in an area that is not in use that Shabbos, one may not decide to sit there and then claim that the repulsive item must be removed.

500. What if the item is in the street?

The exemption applies to any area where people usually walk. This also includes a path leading from the house to the street.

Note: Objects outdoors may not be moved directly or indirectly unless there is an *eiruv*.

501. Must the repulsive item be moved minimally?

No. It may be taken away as far as one wishes, and there is no obligation to put it down at the first opportunity. However, if one puts it down in a place where people do not usually walk, he may not move it again.

502. What if the item could have been removed before Shabbos?

Ideally, one should remove it before Shabbos and not rely on the exemption rule for Shabbos. However if it was left until Shabbos, one may still remove it directly. According to some opinions, it should preferably be removed by a gentile in this case.

Already Holding a Muktzeh Item

503. What are the rules of this situation?

There is a difference between a *kli shemelachto l'issur* and other types of muktzeh items. Regarding a *kli shemelachto l'issur*, if he picked it up with permission (see Question 60), he may carry it to a convenient place and is not required to put it down immediately. Nevertheless, he should not continue to hold it for longer than necessary. According to most opinions, the same leniency applies even if he mistakenly picked it up without permission.

504. What are the rules for other types of muktzeh items?

- If one picked it up with permission (e.g. it is repulsive), he may carry it to a convenient place, see Question 501.
- If one mistakenly picked it up without permission, he must put it down immediately.

505. What if a non-muktzeh item becomes muktzeh while holding it?

According to most opinions, one may carry it to a convenient place and is not required to put it down immediately. For example, if a person peels an orange, the peel is not muktzeh as long as it is still attached to the fruit. However, as soon as it becomes detached it is muktzeh garbage. Nevertheless, one does not need to drop it immediately onto a plate but may carry it to the garbage bin. The same applies to candy wrappers, shells of nuts, eggs, and sunflower seeds, etc.

Cleaning Oneself or an Object

506. What does this rule mean?

As explained in Question 140, dirt is muktzeh since it is usually useless. Nevertheless, one may remove dirt from oneself or from an object although this involves moving something muktzeh. For example, the following activities are permitted even using one's hand:
- Removing dirt from under one's fingernails (taking care not to detach any skin).
- Removing mucus from one's nose or wax from the ear.
- Removing dandruff from a garment.
- Removing a hair, feather, etc., from a garment (but removing dirt or dust that is stuck to a garment is forbidden due to the *melacha* of laundering).
- Rubbing dirt off food (only for immediate use due to the *melacha* of *borer*).
- Scraping food remnants from a plate.
- Wiping dust off a plastic or wooden chair (but removing dust from an upholstered chair is forbidden due to the *melacha* of laundering).
- Wiping condensation off a window (the moisture is muktzeh due to *nolad*, see Question 338).

507. May one remove blades of grass from one's shoe?

No. One may only remove the grass in an indirect or unusual way, e.g. with a knife or tissue.

Human Dignity

508. What are examples of moving muktzeh for human dignity?

- A very wet garment is usually muktzeh (see Question 293). However, if a person has no other suitable clothes to wear, he may put on such a garment for the sake of human dignity. Compare Question 300.
- A roll of toilet paper is muktzeh (see Question 141). However, if a person is in a bathroom and has nothing else to use, he may tear pieces from the roll. He must tear the paper in an unusual way, such as with his elbow, in order to avoid the *melacha* of *korei'a*. The torn pieces may be handled regularly.

Chapter Seventeen
Yom Tov

509. Are the laws of muktzeh on Yom Tov the same as on Shabbos?

Basically, yes. However, in some cases the laws are more lenient and in some they are even more stringent than on Shabbos.

510. Which laws apply on Yom Kippur?

The laws of Shabbos apply. See also Questions 265 and 266.

511. Which laws apply when Yom Tov is on Shabbos?

The laws of Shabbos apply.

512. In which cases are the laws more lenient on Yom Tov?

There are several general cases, as follows:
1. Several *melachos* that are forbidden on Shabbos are permitted on Yom Tov, e.g. lighting a fire and cooking. Items that are connected to these activities are not muktzeh on Yom Tov.
2. Muktzeh items may be moved in order to obtain or prepare food.
3. Mitzvah items.
4. Partially broken items.

513. What are examples of the first case?

- Items connected to *borer* (selecting): peeler, strainer, colander, slotted spoon.
- Items connected to *tochein* (grinding): grater, potato masher, hand mincer, meat chopper, garlic press.
- Items connected to *bishul* (cooking): pots and pans, kettle, cookbook.
- Items connected to *mav'ir* (lighting a fire): candlesticks, candles, wicks, matches, gas knob, electric lamp or radiator (on from before Yom Tov).

All such articles are not muktzeh on Yom Tov since their use is permitted.

514. May these items be moved for any reason?

Yes. This includes the following:
- To use them.
- To use the space where they are lying.
- To reach something behind them.
- In honor of Yom Tov.
- To protect them from loss or damage.

However, one should not move them if there is absolutely no reason to do so, compare Question 19.

515. Is inedible raw food muktzeh?

No, since one may cook it on Yom Tov. For examples, see Question 156. These foods are not muktzeh even if one has no intention to cook them on Yom Tov. For example, one may move them in the refrigerator or freezer in order to reach a different food.

516. Is such food muktzeh toward the end of Yom Tov?

No. Even if there is not enough time left to cook and eat it on Yom Tov, it is not muktzeh. Compare Question 168.

517. Is such food muktzeh when Yom Tov is on *motzai Shabbos*?

When Yom Tov is on *motzai Shabbos*, inedible raw food is muktzeh at the start of Yom Tov. This is because we consider the start of Yom Tov to occur shortly before the termination of Shabbos, and an item that was muktzeh at the start of Shabbos (or Yom Tov) remains muktzeh for the entire day (see Question 448). However, this rule does not apply when Yom Tov is on *motzai Shabbos*, and therefore the food is not muktzeh after the termination of Shabbos.

518. Are any foods muktzeh on Yom Tov?

Yes. The following foods are muktzeh as on Shabbos:
- Forbidden foods, see Question 246.
- Fallen fruit, see Question 309.
- Absolute *nolad*, see Question 338.

519. May one separate *challah* on Yom Tov?

If one makes a dough on Yom Tov, one may separate *challah*. In this situation, the dough is not muktzeh before the separation although it is *tevel*. The separated piece is muktzeh. If the dough was made before Yom Tov, one may not separate *challah* from it on Yom Tov.

520. What are examples of moving muktzeh to obtain or prepare food?
- When it is lying on food that is needed.
- When it is lying on a table or counter and preventing one from eating or preparing food, e.g. leaves of *s'chach* fell onto the succah table.
- When it is mixed with a food, e.g. a bone, shell.

521. May one move such items directly?
Ideally, one should try to move the muktzeh item in an indirect or unusual way (see Question 328). If this is not possible, one may move it directly, but it should be put down at the first opportunity and not handled more than necessary. If the muktzeh item is valuable, one may take it to a safe place before putting it down.

522. What are examples of mitzvah items?
The following are muktzeh on Shabbos but not on Yom Tov even after the mitzvah has been fulfilled:
- A shofar on Rosh Hashanah, see Question 335.
- The *arba minim* on Succos, see Question 330.

523. What is included in partially broken items?
As explained in Question 272, a partially broken item is muktzeh on Shabbos if one might be tempted to repair it. *Chazal* relaxed this decree on Yom Tov, and in certain cases the item may be repaired in a temporary fashion and is therefore not muktzeh.

524. What are examples?

- A detached leg of a table, chair, couch, etc. may be reattached in a temporary way.
- A wheel that fell off a stroller may be reattached loosely.
- A screw that fell out of a glasses frame may be put back loosely.
- A broom-head that fell off the stick may be reattached loosely.

These repairs are permitted if the item is needed for one's enhanced enjoyment of Yom Tov.

525. In which cases are the laws more stringent on Yom Tov?

Items that are ordinary *nolad* are muktzeh on Yom Tov but not on Shabbos. For examples, see Question 343.

526. Why are some of the laws stricter on Yom Tov than on Shabbos?

Since several *melachos* that are forbidden on Shabbos are permitted on Yom Tov, *Chazal* were concerned that people might be overly lenient with the laws of Yom Tov and do prohibited activities. The stricter laws of *nolad* were enacted in order to preserve the *kedusha* of Yom Tov.

527. Do the laws of muktzeh apply on *Chol Hamoed*?

No. All types of muktzeh items may be moved for any reason.

Glossary

Aravos - The willow branches waved on Succos.
Arba minim - The four species waved on Succos.
Ashkenaz - German or Polish Jewry.
Bein hashemashos - *Halachic* twilight.
Beis Hamikdash - The Holy Temple.
Bensch - To recite grace after meals.
Blech - Metal sheet used to cover a fire.
Borer - The *melacha* of selecting or sorting.
Bosis - See Chapter Eleven.
Chadash - Food made from grain that was planted after Pesach and harvested before the following Pesach.
Challah - Portion of dough, originally given to a *cohen*.
Chametz - Leaven, which may not be owned or eaten during Pesach.
Chazal - The Sages.
Chas veshalom - God forbid.
Chol Hamoed - The intermediate days of Pesach and Succos.
Chutz La'aretz - The Diaspora.
Cohen (pl. *cohanim*) - Descendant of Aharon.
Eiruv - An enclosure of a public domain which transforms it into a private one in order to permit objects to be carried on Shabbos.
Eretz Yisroel - The land of Israel.
Erev Pesach - The day before Pesach.
Erev Succos - The day before Succos.
Esrog (pl. *esrogim*) - Citron.
Gemach - Free loan society.

Hadassim - The myrtle branches waved on Succos.

Halacha (pl. *halachos*) - Jewish law.

Havdalah - Prayer recited at the conclusion of Shabbos and Yom Tov to divide between a holy day and a weekday.

Kabbalas Shabbos - The prayers recited at the beginning of Shabbos.

Kedusha - Sanctity.

Kesuba - Marriage contract.

Kitniyos - Certain vegetables and seeds that may not be eaten on Pesach according to Ashkenazic custom.

Kli shemelachto le'heter - See Question 17.

Kli shemelachto l'issur - See Chapter Three.

Korei'a - The *melacha* of tearing.

Lulav - The palm branch waved on Succos.

Mayim acharonim - Washing before *bensching*.

Melacha (pl. *melachos*) - Activity forbidden on Shabbos by the Torah.

Mikveh - A ritual immersion pool.

Mitzvah (pl. *mitzvos*) - A commandment.

Mishna Brura - The classic and accepted *halachic* work on the daily and holiday laws, written by Rav Yisroel Meir HaCohen Kagan (1839-1933).

Motzai Shabbos - The evening after Shabbos.

Muktzeh machmas chisaron kis - See Chapter Five.

Muktzeh machmas gufo - See Chapter Six.

Nagel vasser - Ritual washing of the hands performed when waking up.

Navi (pl. *nevi'im*) - A Prophet.

Nolad - See Chapter Ten.

Passul - Invalid.

S'chach - The roofing material for a succah.
Sefer (pl. *sefarim*) - A Jewish book.
Sephard - Spanish, Portugese, or North African Jewry.
Shaatnez - A forbidden combination of wool and linen in a garment.
Shechita - Ritual slaughter.
Shemini Atzeres - The eighth day of Succos.
Shemos - The book of Exodus.
Shtender - Podium.
Simchas Torah - The eighth day of Succos in *Eretz Yisroel*, the ninth day in *Chutz La'aretz*.
Tallis katan - Small four cornered garment.
Tefach (pl. *tefachim*) - Linear measure (8cm)
Tefillin - Phylacteries.
Tevel - Untithed produce of *Eretz Yisroel*.
Terumah - Tithes.
Tzedaka - Charity.
Tzitzis - Four cornered garment with fringes; the fringes.
Yad soledes bo - Literally, the degree of heat from which the hand withdraws. This refers to the critical temperature at which the *melacha* of *bishul* can take place.
Yeshayahu - The prophet Isiah.
Zemiros - Songs of praise sung on Shabbos.

Index

Acid 156
Advil 64
Air conditioner vents 41
Air conditioning water107, 149, 165
Air freshener spray 23
Animal 56, 75
Ant 75, 141
Antibiotics 64
Antique *sefer* 23
Apple peel 71
Apple pits 71
Appliance, on that is often off 32, 40
Apricot pits 71
Aquarium 76
Aravos 103
Arba minim 103, 166
Arm-rest, detached 90
Artificial grass 59
Aspirin 64
Astronomy book 33
Aveida 54
Avocado peel 71
Baby, new-born 107
Baby-wipes 98
Back of the hand, moving muktzeh with 141
Bag containing money 111
Bag containing muktzeh and non-muktzeh items 125, 154
Baked goods, from which challah was not separated 83, 84
Ball
 playing with 25, 58, 148
Ball of string/thread/wool . 56
Balloon 27
Banana peel 71
Band-Aid 67
Basket, animal 76
Battery 29

Battery operated toy 26
Battery operated toy, broken 145
Beads, threading 25
Beans, not cooked 60
Bed linen 23
Bed-sheet, soiled 98
Bed-sheet, wet 97
Beets, not cooked 60
Before Shabbos, item not ready for use 143
Bein hashemashos,
 significance in making a *bosis* 116, 144
Bicycle 25, 29
Bin, garbage 32
Binder, loose-leaf 49
Biology book 33
Bird 56, 75
Bird cage 76
Birth certificate 49
Blank notebook 48
Bleach 56
Blech 23
Blow-dryer 29
Blowing muktzeh 75, 141
Bone, removing from mouth 71
Bones 70, 122, 137, 153, 158, 166
 edible to animals .. 72, 108
Books, secular 23
Booster seat, using thick book 32, 33
Bosis
 bag containing money . 111
 definition 110
 drawer containing pans 112
 forgot to remove muktzeh 113
 from sunset until nightfall 116, 144
 intentional placement .. 113

moving 111
muktzeh fell onto item 113
muktzeh placed by child 118, 121
muktzeh placed by guest 120
muktzeh placed by owner 120
muktzeh placed by wife 121
muktzeh placed on a public item 121
muktzeh placed on a shared item 121
muktzeh placed on Shabbos 117
muktzeh removed on Shabbos 112, 143
muktzeh serving non-muktzeh 110
non-muktzeh above muktzeh 110
temporary 118, 119
time of placement 116, 144
to a *bosis* 112
to muktzeh and non-muktzeh. 125, 150, 154
valuable muktzeh item placed 122
Bottle of wine, sealed 62
Bowls 22
Branches of a tree 58, 148
Broken glass 156
Broken item 56
Broken utensil 68, 88, 108, 145, 166
Broom, pushing muktzeh with 137
Broom-head 94, 167
Brush, clothes 29
Brush, paint 56
Brush, shoe 29
Burning coal 156
Button 94
Cage, bird 76
Calculator 29, 137
Camera, tilting off chair .. 129

Can of food 62
Can opener 62
Candle 57, 164
Candlestick tray 112, 126
Candlesticks on table with challos 116, 125
Candy wrapper ... 70, 72, 160
Car door 42
Carrot peel 71
Cellphone 46
Cellphone, broken 68
Cellphone, moving to protect 138
Chadash 87
Chair
 arm-rest became detached 90
 hammer left on 36
 leg broke off 89, 167
 muktzeh placed onto ... 112
 tilting muktzeh off 128
Chalk 29
Challah 84, 165
Challos
 muktzeh food on top of 115
 on table with candlesticks 125
Chametz on Pesach 82, 86, 165
Chametz utensils
 on Pesach 52
Check book 49
Cheese container 73
Chemicals, dangerous 156
Chicken and milk mixture . 85
Chicken bones 108
Chicken, raw 60
Child
 designating an item 80
 holding muktzeh 138
 passing *kli shemelachto l'issur* to 36
 placed muktzeh 121
 placed muktzeh on Shabbos 117
 playing with muktzeh toys 24

removed muktzeh on Shabbos........ 112, 143
Chol Hamoed........... 21, 167
Clearing garbage off table. 74
Clementine peel 71
Clock, wall...................... 51
Closed bottle of wine 62
Closet, handle fell off ..90, 91
Clothes brush................... 29
Clothing 22
Clothing, for sale 52
Coal, burning 156
Coat with muktzeh in pocket 131
Coffee........................... 61
Colander 164
Comb.............................. 29
Condensation, wiping off window 161
Container
  placing under dripping air conditioner 152
Container, placing under dripping air conditioner 150
Contract......................... 49
Cookbook 32, 164
Cookie crumbs 63
Cord, electric 45
Corkscrew 62
Cosmetics....................... 56
Couch
  leg broke off 89
Couch, leg broke off....... 167
Cover of garbage bin...... 122
Cover, pot 31
Covering, to protect muktzeh 37, 138
Cream............................. 56
Credit card 49
Crockpot 44
Crumbs........................... 63
Crystal 51
Cucumber peel................ 71
Cup, disposable............... 73
Cupcake wrappers 72, 160
Cups.............................. 22

Cutlery........................... 22
Cutlery, disposable 73
Dandruff 161
Dangerous item 155
Dead rodent 157
Decorations, succah.101, 102
Dental floss 56
Deodorant....................... 22
Deodorant stick............... 56
Designation
  changing muktzeh item into non-muktzeh 77
  doing before Shabbos .. 77
  of a child.................... 80
  of a gentile................. 80
  of *kli shemelachto l'issur*81
  of *muktzeh machmas chisaron kis*............. 81
  rock as a doorstop....... 77
Diaper, dirty 70, 157
Dirt, cleaning off garment 161
Dirty pan/pot................. 158
Dish containing peels or shells 124, 137
Dishcloth........................ 23
Dishcloth, wet.................. 97
Dishwasher door 42
Disposable cup........... 69, 73
Disposable napkin, using to wipe up a spill............ 153
Disposable pan 30
Disposable plate, putting peels or sheels onto............ 153
Disposable plate/cutlery ... 73
Disposable tablecloth 74
Dog, seeing eye 75
Doll............................... 26
Door
  became detached from piece of furniture 90
  garbage attached to ...124
  handle fell off 90
  muktzeh hanging on it 127
  opening with a screwdriver 29
Door of refrigerator

containing muktzeh and
   non-muktzeh items 128
Door, car 42
Door, dishwasher 42
Door, dryer 41, 147
Door, handle fell off 91
Door, oven 41
Door, refrigerator 43
Door, washing machine 42
Doorknob
   became detached from
      piece of furniture 90
Doorpost
   mezuza fell off 53
Doorstop
   designating rock as 77
Drapes, succah 102
Drawer
   containing garbage bin 123
   containing money and
      tissues 126, 137
   containing muktzeh and
      non-muktzeh items 115,
      125, 128, 154
   putting muktzeh into on
      Shabbos 150, 151
   removed non-muktzeh
      items 120
Drawer containing pans .. 112
Drawer, non-removable .. 135
Drawer, removable 134
Dresser with several removable
   drawers 135
Dried flower arrangement . 59
Drinks 22
Drinks, for sale 52
Driving licence 49
Dryer door 41, 147
Dust, cleaning off
   chair/garment 161
Dustpan 124, 137, 138
Ear plugs 67
Egg slicer 23
Egg, freshly laid 21, 107, 165
Eggs 61

Elbow, moving muktzeh with
   140
Electric cord 45
Electric kettle 44
Empty container 73
Empty pot 28, 150
Envelope 49
Eraser 29
Erev Pesach, chametz 86
Esrog 53, 104
   smelling 104
Eyeglasses
   lens fell out 93
   screw fell out 92, 167
Fan 32, 40
Faucet knob, fell off 91
Faucet, hot water 146
Feather
   removing from garment 161
Fiction book 33
File, nail 29
Fingernails
   removing dirt from
      underneath 161
Fish 56, 60, 75
Flashlight 29
Floor rag 29
Flour 56
Flower 59
Flower arrangement 51
Flowerpot 59
Foil 56
Food
   for sale 52
   inedible 60
   placing on candlestick tray
      126
   removing dirt from 161
Food 22
Food leftovers ... 63, 137, 161
Food on Yom Kippur 87
Food, frozen (edible) 62
Foot, moving muktzeh with
   .... 140, 141
Forearm
   moving muktzeh with .. 141

Index

Forgot to remove muktzeh 113
Found article 54
Framed picture 50
Freezer
    containing muktzeh and non-muktzeh food 115, 140
Frozen food, edible 62
Fruit salad, juice that seeped out while preparing 100
Fruit, fell off a tree .. 98, 145, 165
Fruit, unripe 62, 144
Fruits
    juice that seeped out ... 99
Furniture 23
    door broke off 90
    leg broke off 89, 167
    needs skill to repair 89
Games involving writing 25
Garbage 56, 70, 153
Garbage bag 123
Garbage bin 32, 122, 123, 153
Garbage bin cover 122
Garbage bin in a drawer . 123
Garbage, smelly 157
Garbage, unsightly 157
Garden tools 29
Garlic peel 71
Garlic press 164
Garment
    removing dirt from 161
    using to wipe up a spill 151
Garment containing *shaatnez* 82, 87, 165
Garment, dirty 95
Garment, wet 94, 147, 162
    changing out of 96
    wearing 95
Gentile
    asking to move a repulsive item 157
    asking to move *kli shemelachto l'issur* .. 38
    bringing valuable item inside 142

designating a rock as a doorstop 80
moving muktzeh 142
passing *kli shemelachto l'issur* to 35
placed muktzeh on Shabbos 117
removed muktzeh on Shabbos 112, 143
touched wine 85
Geography book 33
Glass, broken 156
Glasses
    lens fell out 93
    screw fell out 92, 167
Glasses, reading 22
Glue 56
Graf .... See Repulsive item
Grapefruit peel 71
Grapefruit, juice that seeped out 99
Grapes 146
    juice that seeped out ... 99
Grass 58
Grass, removing from shoe 161
Grater 29, 164
Ground coffee 61
Hadassim 103
Hair
    removing from garment 161
Hairbrush 29
Hammer 28
    cracking nuts with .. 34, 35
    left on a chair 36
    left outside in the rain .. 37
Hand, back of, moving muktzeh with 141
Handle
    fell off cabinet 90
    fell off door 90, 91
Heater 141
Hot water faucet 146
Hotplate 43
House, model - building ... 25
Ice cream
    making on Yom Tov 109

muktzeh food next to. 137
muktzeh food on top of115, 140
Ice cream wrappers .. 72, 160
Ice cubes
   making on Yom Tov ... 109
Ice that melted 109
Identity card 49
Important item
   determining *bosis* status
      .... 125, 126
   in drawer with other
      muktzeh item 120
   muktzeh machmas chisaron kis......................... 49
   on desk with muktzeh in
      drawer 134
Indirect movement 136
   in the usual way 138
   scraping leftovers into
      garbage 63
   to protect muktzeh 138
Inedible pits/seeds 70
Insect 75
   removing from table75, 141
Instruction leaflet 32
Interlocking toys 27
Ironing board 29
Item changing status
   during Shabbos 20
Item one intends as a gift. 54
Item one intends returning to store 54
Item placed with no specific intention 114
Jacket
   hanging on a tree branch58
   muktzeh in pocket 131
Jewelry 22
Jigsaw 26
Kesuba 49
Kettle 164
Kettle, electric 44
Keys 23
Kitniyos 86
Kli shemelachto le'heter

moving 23
Kli shemelachto l'issur
   blocking one's way 36
   breaks on Shabbos 145
   covering to protect 37
   definition 28
   gentile moving to protect it
      38
   having a secondary use 28
   item that assists in doing a forbidden activity 32
   item that holds muktzeh32
   left on a chair 36
   moving 34
   moving for later use..... 36
   moving indirectly 37
   moving to make room tidy
      38
   moving to protect 37
   moving to use 34
   moving to use its place 36
   passing to a child 36
   passing to a gentile 35
   passing to someone 35
   putting down as soon as possible 37
   putting down if picked up
     159
   putting in empty drawer on Shabbos 150
   reading material 32
   using as a paperweight 30
   using in order to protect it
      38
Knee, moving muktzeh with
  140
Knot, tying 25
Lamp, table 45
Later in day, moving *kli shemelachto le'heter* 23
Leaf 18, 56, 58
Leather shoes on Yom Kippur
   87
Leftovers (food) 63, 137, 161
Leg, broke off a piece of furniture 89, 167

Index

Lemon peel 71
Lemon, juice that seeped out
.... 100
Lens, fell out of glasses frame
.... 93
Linen, bed 23
Liquid soap 23
Loose-leaf binder 49
Lulav 103
Magnet 27
Marbles, playing with outside
.... 25
Masher, potato 164
Matches 57, 156, 164
Math book 33
Mayim Acharonim 74
Meat and milk mixture 82, 165
Meat bones 108
Meat, raw 60, 61
Medical text book 33
Medicine 56, 64, 156
Melon peel 71
Melon seeds 70
Melted liquid 109
Merchandise 52
Mezuza 53
Microwave, placing item on top
of 19
Milk, fresh from a cow 107, 165
Milk, mother's 107
Mincer 164
Mixture of chicken and milk 85
Mixture of meat and milk. 82, 165
Moldy food 70
Money 56
   child holding 139
   in a bag 111
   in drawer with tissues 126, 137
   left in pocket 130
Mop 29
Mother's milk 107
Mouse, dead 157
Moving indirectly 136
Moving muktzeh

indirectly 136
indirectly to protect it .. 138
with one's body 140
Moving with one's body ... 136
Mucus 161
Muktzeh
   meaning 17
   origin 17
Muktzeh machmas chisaron kis
   breaks on Shabbos 145
   definition 47
   documents 49
   inexpensive item 48
   item one intends returning
      to store 54
   merchandise 52
   moving 47
   ornament 51
   Pesach utensils 51
   picture 50
Muktzeh machmas gufo
   animals 75
   broken utensils 68
   definition 55
   disposable items 73
   garbage 70
   inedible food 60
   leftover food 63
   medicine 64
   money 56
   moving 55
   plants 58
   useless items 56
Muktzeh machmas issur
   broken glasses 92
   broken stroller 91
   broken utensil 88
   chametz on Pesach 86
   definition 82
   fallen fruit 98
   juice that seeped out of
      fruit 99
   meat and milk 84
   moving 82
   shaatnez 87
   tevel 83

treif food 85
wet garment 94
Muktzeh machmas mitzvah
   arba minim 103
   definition 101
   moving 101
   s'chach 103
   succah decorations 101
Musical instruments 26
Nagel Vasser 74
Nail file 29
Nails (building) 29
Napkin, paper, using to wipe up a spill 153
Needle 28, 156
New utensil 88
New-born baby 107
Newspaper 33
No reason, moving *kli shemelachto le'heter* 23, 164
Nolad
   absolute *nolad* 107
   definition 106
   moving 106
   ordinary *nolad* 108
   Yom Tov 167
Non-removable drawer ... 135
Noodles, not cooked 60
Notebook 48
Notes, Torah 22
Novel 33
Nutcracker, cracking nuts with 35
Nuts, cracking with a hammer 34
Onion peel 71
Orange peel 71, 160
Orange, juice that seeped out 99
Organizing house on Shabbos 18
Origin, muktzeh 17
Ornament 23, 51
Oven door 29, 41
Packages 70
Pad, writing 48

Page, torn 24
Paint 56
Paintbrush 29, 56
Pan, containing food 31
Pan, dirty 38, 158
Pan, empty 30, 36
Pans 164
Pans in a drawer 112
Paper
   designating as a bookmark 79
Paper cup/plate 73
Paper napkin, using to wipe up a spill 153
Paper, designating as a bookmark 77
Paperweight
   using a *kli shemelachto l'issur* as 30
   using telephone directory 32
Paracetamol 64
Passport 49
Patch pocket 131
Peach peel 71
Pear peel 71
Pear pits 71
Pebbles, child designating as a toy 80
Peeler 29, 164
Peeling fruit with muktzeh peel 72, 124, 137, 160
Peels ... 70, 71, 122, 153, 158
   edible to animals .. 72, 108
   making a dish a *bosis*.124, 137
Pen 30
Perfume 22
Pesach utensils
   during the year 51
Pet 75
   causing a disturbance . 142
Pet food 60
Petit fours wrappers . 72, 160
Picture, framed 50
Picture, straightening on wall 50

Index

Pineapple peel 71
Pins............................. 156
Pit
   edible to animals .. 72, 108
   removing from mouth .. 71
Pits, edible 70
Plank of wood
   designating to use in a game...................... 77
Plastic bag, putting garbage into 153
Plasticine........................ 27
Plate, broken 68
Plate, chipped 68
Plate, disposable 73
Plate, disposable, putting peels or sheels onto 153
Plate, putting peels or shells onto 153
Plates 22
Play-doh.......................... 27
Plum peel 71
Pocket
   forgot muktzeh in 130
   leaving muktzeh in 130, 132
   left muktzeh in 131
Pomegranate, juice that seeped out 99
Postage stamp 50, 81
Pot
   holding while serving last portion................... 39
   storing food in........30, 81
Pot cover........................ 31
Pot, containing food......... 31
Pot, dirty 38, 158
Pot, empty 28, 36, 150
Potato, raw................56, 60
Pots............................. 164
Potted plant.................... 59
Protecting item
   a gentile moving... 38, 142
   moving a *kli shemelachto le'heter* 23
   moving a *kli shemelachto l'issur*...................... 37
   moving indirectly........138
   moving with one's body 140
Protection of Shabbos, laws of muktzeh..................... 18
Pumpkin seeds................. 70
Purse............................. 32
   containing money.......122
Purse left on chair
   bosis 127
Putting down
   kli shemelachto l'issur that picked up..............159
   repulsive item that picked up.........................159
Pyrex dish 30
Quince, raw.................... 60
Raddish peel................... 71
Radiator.................. 44, 164
Rag, floor....................... 29
Rag, using to wipe up a spill 153
Rag, wet........................ 97
Rain 107
   gentile bringing in valuable items to protect 142
   moving *kli shemelachto l'issur* to protect from 37
   moving muktzeh indirectly to protect from 138
Raisins..........................146
Rattle 26
Raw eggs....................... 61
Raw fish 61
Raw food placed on blech close to Shabbos 147
Raw foods............... 60, 164
Raw meat 61
Raw potato 56
Red-hot metal................156
Refrigerator
   handle fell off 90
   placing medicine into ... 65
Refrigerator door............. 43
   containing muktzeh and non-muktzeh items. 128
Removable drawer 134

Repulsive item 157
   in the street.............. 158
   subjective................. 157
Rice, not cooked.............. 60
Ring, placing on candlestick tray 126
Rock, designating as a doorstop 77, 79
Roll of floss/foil/toilet paper 56
Rolling up disposable tablecloth 74
Ruler 29
Salad, juice that seeped out while preparing 100
Sales catalogue, using as a booster seat................ 33
Sashimi........................... 61
Saw................................. 29
Scale 29
S'chach................. 103, 166
   blown out of position.. 103
   falls down................. 103
Scissors.......................... 29
Scotch tape 56
Scraps of food................. 70
Screw, fell out of glasses frame 92, 167
Screwdriver 29
Screws............................ 29
Secular books 23
Seeds, inedible................ 70
Seeing eye dog 75
Sefarim.......................... 22
Sefarim for sale............... 52
Sefer, antique 23
Sellotape......................... 56
Sewing machine, cloth covering................... 111
Shaatnez garment 82, 87, 165
Shaking muktzeh off a *bosis* 127, 130
Shechita knife 47
Sheet of paper 48
Shelling eggs/nuts ... 72, 124, 137, 160
Shells 70, 122, 137, 153, 158, 166
Shemini Atzeres, succah decorations 101
Ship, model - building 25
Shirt, muktzeh in pocket.. 131
Shoe brush...................... 29
Shoe, removing grass from 161
Shoes on Yom Kippur....... 87
Shofar 105, 166
Shoulder, moving muktzeh with 140
Shtender, shul - muktzeh item placed on 121
Sifter.............................. 29
Silver polish..................... 56
Simchas Torah, succah decorations 101
Sitting on muktzeh 142
Sleeping pills 66
Slotted spoon 164
Smelling
   a growing flower 59
   esrog........................ 104
   garbage.................... 122
   hadassim 103
Smelly garbage.............. 157
Snow............................ 108
Snuff 22
Soap, bar....................... 57
Soap, liquid 23
Soda bottle, empty 73
Soiled bed-sheet 98
Spider web..................... 76
Spill
   using garment to wipe up 151
Spill, using paper napkin to wipe up 153
Spill, using rag to wipe up 153
Spinner........................... 23
Sponge, wet.................... 97
Spray, air freshener 23
Squeegee....................... 29
Stamp, postage.......... 50, 81
Staples 56

Index

Steel wool 29
Sticks............................. 56
Straightening picture on wall 50
Strainer......................... 164
Strawberries, juice that seeped out 99
String 56
Stroller.......................... 23
Stroller, wheel fell off 91, 167
Succah decorations 101
   fell down 102, 144
   removed on *Chol Hamoed* 102
   with words of Torah... 102
Succah drapes 102
Suction hook, fell off side of refrigerator 91
Suitcase
   containing muktzeh and non-muktzeh items 115, 125, 128, 154
   removed non-muktzeh items 120
Sunflower seeds .. 70, 72, 160
Sushi 61
Sweeping floor 124, 137, 138
Table lamp 45
Table leg broke off ... 89, 167
Tablecloth 23
   shaking 74
   wet........................... 97
   with candlesticks on ... 113
Tableware 22
Tableware for sale 52
Tallis or *tallis katan* without *tzitzis*....................... 87
Tape measure................. 29
Tea-bag 61
Tefillin, removing from tallis 36
Telephone directory 32
Telephone, broken - designating as a toy 77
Temporary *bosis*............. 119
Terumah....................... 84
Tevel..................... 82, 165
Theft

moving *kli shemelachto l'issur* to protect from 37
Thermometer 67
Thorns.......................... 156
Thread.......................... 56
Tidying room
   moving a *kli shemelachto l'issur*..................... 23
Tidying room, moving a *kli shemelachto l'issur* 38
Tilting muktzeh off a *bosis* 127
Tissues in drawer with money 126, 137
Toaster.......................... 29
Toilet paper............. 56, 162
Tools 29, 156
Toothbrush 29
Toothpaste..................... 56
Torah notes.................... 22
Torn page 24
Touching muktzeh object 18, 20, 58
Towel, wet..................... 97
Toy, battery operated 26
Toy, battery operated, broken 145
Toy, wind-up 26
Toy, with interlocking pieces 27
Toys................... 23, 137
Toys, muktzeh - children playing with 24
Tray, candlestick 112, 126
Tree 56, 58
   removing ball from 148
   sitting on roots........... 58
Treif food 85
Treif utensil 88
Tricycle......................... 25
Trousers, muktzeh in pocket 131
Tweezers 29
Tylenol 64
Tzedaka box 32
Umbrella 29
Unripe fruit/vegetable 62, 144
Unsightly garbage 157

Untithed produce............. 83
Using muktzeh object....... 19
Using place
   moving a *kli shemelachto*
     le'heter................... 23
Utensil made by a gentile 108
Utensil, broken...68, 88, 108, 145, 166
Utensil, new..................... 88
Utensil, treif..................... 88
Vacuum cleaner 29
Valuable item................... 51
   broken....................... 68
   child holding 139
   gentile bringing inside 142
   moving indirectly to protect
     138
   putting in empty drawer on
     Shabbos................ 151
   tilting off chair........... 129
   tilting onto a pillow 151
Value
   determining *bosis* status 125
Vegetable, unripe 62, 144
Vents, air conditioner 41
Vitamins.......................... 66
Wall clock........................ 51
Wallet............................. 32
   containing money 122
Wallet left on chair
   bosis........................ 127
Washing machine
   touching..................... 18
Washing machine door..... 42
Washing powder 56
Watch......................22, 45
Watch, calculator............. 45
Watch, stopped........ 45, 141

Water, from air conditioner
   ....107, 149, 165
Watermelon peel............. 71
Watermelon seeds........... 70
Watermelon, juice that seeped
   out............................ 99
Wet bed-sheet................ 97
Wet garment 94, 147, 162
   changing out of........... 96
   wearing 95
Wet rag/sponge.............. 97
Wet tablecloth 97
Wet towel/dishcloth......... 97
Wheel
   fell off stroller 91, 167
Window, wiping condensation
   off...........................161
Wind-up toy 26
Wine of idolatry .. 82, 85, 165
Wine touched by a gentile 85
Wool 56
Wrapping paper 49
Writing pad 48
Writing, games that involve 25
Yeast............................. 60
Yoghurt container............ 73
Yom Kippur 163
Yom Kippur, food 87
Yom Kippur, leather shoes 87
Yom Tov
   broken items 166
   making ice cream/ice cubes
    109
   nolad.......................167
   raw food 164
   restrictions 163
   separating *challah* 165

Hebrew Sources

ספרים המובאים במקורות

ארחות שבת - הג"ר ש.י. גלבר והג"ר י.מ. רובין.
הלכות מוקצה - הג"ר ש.ב. כהן (ארטסקרול).
הלכות שבת בשבת (חלק ב) - הג"ר מ.מ. קארפ.
זכור ושמור - הרב פ.א. פאלק.
חוט שני - הג"ר נ. קרליץ.
טלטולי שבת - הגרי"פ באדנער (אנגלית).
לוח המוקצה - הגרי"י בן צור, תשס"ו.
נחלת ישראל - הגרי"נ קרויס.
פסקי הגרי"ש - קובץ הלכות להגרי"ש אלישיב.
שבות יצחק (חלק א) - הג"ר י. דרזי.
שלמי יהונתן (חלק ג, בירורי הלכות) - הגר"י בן צור.
שמירת שבת כהלכתה - הג"ר י.י. נויווירט, תש"ע.

פרק א - יסודות כלליים

[1] חיי"א כלל סו סימן א בא"ד ונ"ל להוסיף. [2] נחמיה יג:טו, שבת קכג/ב, ערה"ש סימן רמג סעיף א-ג, פסחים מז/ב. [3] רמב"ם הלכות שבת פכ"ד הלכה יב-יג וראב"ד שם. [4] סימן שח סעיף מב, רמ"א סעיף ג. [5] שש"כ פכ"ב סעיף לג ע"פ מ"פ סימן שח ס"ק פב. ועיין מ"ב בסימן שט ס"ק טו ומבואר בשעה"צ שהשלחן אינו מוקצה, וחשש רק לגבי המעות. [7] מ"ב בהקדמה לסימן שח. [8] סימן שח סעיף ב ומ"ב סק"ח, סעיף ד ומ"ב ס"ק כג, נחלת ישראל עמוד קלו אות ב. [9] שם. [10] סימן שי סעיף ג, ז, סימן שח סעיף כז ומ"ב ס"ק קיג-קיד. [11] סימן שכב סעיף א. [12] שש"כ פכ"א סעיף ח, מבקשי תורה עמוד תנד (לו) בשם הגריש"א והגרח"ק. [13] ד"מ סימן תקמד סעיף ב, מ"ב סימן תרלח ס"ק יד.

פרק ב - כלים שאינם מוקצה

[14] סימן שח סעיף ד. [15] ספרים ואוכלים, שם. כלי סעודה, מ"ב ס"ק כג. בגדים ותכשיטים, שש"כ פ"כ סעיף פג. בושם וטבק ומשקפיים, מבית לוי ח"ו עמוד מו. שעון, ארחות שבת פי"ט סעיף פז. [16] עיין מ"ב סימן שט ס"ק יג, חיי"א כלל סה סימן ג פן ז וכלל סו סימן ב. [17] פשוט. [18] סימן שח סעיף ד, ומ"ש לסדר החדר עיין ארחות שבת פי"ט סעיף פד. [19] ארחות שבת שם, ערוה"ש סעיף טו. [20] להרגעת עצביו שבת ח"ב עמוד שכה. לנדנד סטנדר עיין נחלת ישראל עמוד קמו, ועיין מעשה איש ח"ב עמוד קו שאמר החזו"א שמילוי רצונו של אדם הוי לצורך. [21] לוח המוקצה מהדורא אנגלית ערך ספרים עתיקים. [22] אז נדברו ח"ב סימן סח. [23] עיין שלמי יהודה פ"א הערה כ בשם הגריש"א והגר"ב זילבר להתיר, וכ"כ בהלכות מוקצה להגרשב"כ

עמוד 77, ועיין ארחות שבת פי"ט סעיף קכג בשם החזו"א לאסור, וע"ע מאור השבת ח"ב עמוד תרכו.   [הקדמה למשחקים] עיין כה"ח סימן שח ס"ק רנט וסימן שלח ס"ק לט, מ"ב סימן תקיח סק"ט.   [24] מ"ב סימן שמג סק"ג, וגיל שלש מוזכר בספר חינוך הבנים למצוות להגרי"י נויבירט סעיף לח, וע"ע חינוך בהלכה להגרש"ב כהן עמוד 8 שכתב עד גיל ארבע.   [25] לענין גולות עיין סימן שלח סעיף ה ומ"ב סק"כ. לענין משחקי בניה עיין זכור ושמור כותב עמוד 9. לענין מחרוזות עיין שש"כ פט"ז סעיף כב. לענין כותב עיין חיי"א כלל לח סימן יא. לענין כדור עיין מ"ב סימן שח ס"ק קנח.   [26] שש"כ פט"ז סעיף יח, טלטולי שבת עמוד 24.   [27] טלטולי שבת עמוד 25, שש"כ פט"ז הערה סז בשם הגרשז"א, ארחות שבת פי"ט סעיף נו ועיי"ש הערה פ האם מותר לטלטלו לצורך גו'מ.   [28] לענין רעשן עיין טלטולי שבת עמוד 26 בשם הגרמ"פ שאינו מוקצה, ועיין שש"כ פט"ז סעיף ב שהוא מוקצה, ועיין ארחות שבת פי"ט הערה עח.   [29] ארחות שבת פי"ט הערה עז וסעיף פח, טלטולי שבת עמוד 56.   [30] ארחות שבת פ"ח סעיף נו ופי"ט סעיף נג אות ג.   [31] שש"כ פט"ז סעיף יד.   [32] לוח המוקצה ערך ווקי טוקי (בחלק המשחקים).   [33] עיין ארחות שבת פ"ח סעיף נט והערה פו, ופי"ט סעיף נה, שש"כ פט"ז סעיף יט.   [34] שש"כ פט"ז סעיף ז, ארחות שבת פ"ח סעיף סט.   [35] שש"כ פט"ז סעיף יג.   [36] לוח המוקצה ערך מגנט, הלכות מוקצה עמוד 90.

פרק ג - כלי שמלאכתו לאיסור

[37] סימן שח סעיף ג, מ"ב סק"י.   [38] מ"ב סימן שח ס"ק לד, ועיין ארחות שבת פי"ט הערה כא, הלכות מוקצה עמוד 15 והערה 14.   [39] סעיף ג, סעיף יא, מ"ב סק"כ.   [40] לוח המוקצה.   [41] שם.   [42] ארחות שבת פי"ט הערה כא בשם החזו"א, שלמי יהודה עמוד יח בשם הגריש"א, לוח המוקצה ערך מברג.   [43] שלמי יהודה פי"ב סעיף י בשם הגריש"א שמקיל, וכ"כ נחלת ישראל ריש עמוד קסא, וכן נוטה בלוח המוקצה ערך לורדים (הערה 484). ועיי"ש בשם הגרצ"ו להחמיר. וע"ע מגילת ספר פמ"ו אות ז שדינו כבסיס לדיו שהוא מוקצה מחמת גופו.   [44] ארחות שבת פי"ט סוף הערה כא.   [45] חוט שני ח"ג עמוד פו ד"ה ואמנם, ארחות שבת פי"ט סעיף לח אות ג, שלמי יהודה פ"ו הערה יב בשם הגריש"א.   [46] בה"ל סימן שח סעיף ג סד"ה קורדום, הלכות מוקצה עמוד 192.   [47] לוח המוקצה ערך תבנית אפיה, ארחות שבת פי"ט סעיף לט.   [48] מ"ב סימן שח ס"ק כו, גר"ז סעיף כב, ועיין נחלת ישראל עמוד קפ ד"ה בהאי שחוקר אם מותר לטלטלו שלא לצורך כלל.   [49] הלכות מוקצה עמוד 192, נחלת ישראל עמוד קעט.   [50] כן נראה, וע"ע נחלת ישראל עמוד קפא.   [51] חוט שני ח"ג עמוד צא אות ג,

ד, שבת בשבת ח"ב פכ"ד סעיף יז. [52] חוט שני עמוד צא, נחלת ישראל עמוד קף בשם הגריש"א. [53] ארנק, רמ"א סימן שי סעיף ז. מדריך טלפון, שש"כ פ"כ סעיף יז והערה מה בשם הגרשז"א, שבות יצחק עמוד יח בשם הגריש"א, חוט שני ח"ג עמוד פב, טלטולי שבת עמוד 139 (וע"ע שבת בשבת עמוד שנה בשם הגריש"א שאינו מוקצה, וכ"כ בפסקי הגרי"ש עמוד קלג). דף הוראות, שבת בשבת ח"ב פכ"ד סעיף כב. מאוורר, אג"מ ח"ג סימן מט, שש"כ פי"ג סעיף מ, ארחות שבת פי"ט סעיף ה. [54] שש"כ פ"כ סעיף יז, ארחות שבת פי"ט סעיף סט הערה צח. [55] איל משולש שטרי הדיוטות פ"ב הערה לד בשם הגרמ"פ והגרנ"ק, וע"ע שש"כ פכ"ט הערה קכד בשם הגרשז"א שנוטה לומר שמותר לקרותו ואינו מוקצה אמנם עיין שם פ"כ סעיף יז דהוי כשמל"א, ועיין ארחות שבת פכ"ב הערה רכג. [56] טלטולי שבת עמוד 138, ועיי"ש בתשובת הגרמ"פ אות כה, ועיין שש"כ פכ"ט הערה קיג* ופ"כ סעיף יז, אלא שמותר לעיין בה אם נהנים. [57] סימן שז סעיף יז ומ"ב ס"ק סה, סימן שח סעיף נ ומ"ב ס"ק קסד. [58] סימן שז סעיף טז, ארחות שבת פכ"ב סעיף קמה, הלכות מוקצה עמוד 183. [59] מ"ב סימן שז ס"ק סג-סד, קצה"ש סימן קז ס"ק מג, ארחות שבת פכ"ב סעיף קמד, ועיין לוח המוקצה ערך עיתון - רובו חדשות עם הערה שכתב שאין לו חשיבות כלי והוי מוקצה מחמת גופו, טלטולי שבת עמוד 141, הלכות שבת השייכים לבית (רשב"כ) עמוד 62. [60] סימן שח סעיף ג, סימן שיא סעיף ח. [61] מ"ב סימן שח ס"ק יב. [62] שם. [63] עיין שעה"צ ס"ק יג דמשמע שיש לטרוח, וכן דייק בארחות שבת פי"ט הערה לג, וכן פסק הגרצ"ו הובא בשלמי יהונתן ח"ג עמוד קסח. ועיין טלטולי שבת פסקי הגרמ"פ אות ה שא"צ לטרוח הרבה, וכ"כ בקצה"ש סימן קח ס"ק יד. ולענין שאלה משכן כ"כ בשלמי יהונתן שם בשם הגרצ"ו, וכ"כ בארחות שבת שם סעיף טו. [64] פשוט. [65] שש"כ פ"כ סעיף ט והערה כא, ארחות שבת פי"ט סעיף טז, חוט שני ח"ג עמוד עח. [66] ארחות שבת פי"ט סעיף יב, נחלת ישראל עמוד תצ, שלמי יהונתן ח"ג סימן יג, וע"ע שבת בשבת פכ"ד סעיף ט. [67] ארחות שבת פי"ט סעיף י, חוט שני עמוד פא ד"ה מ"מ, וע"ע נחלת ישראל עמוד קנו. [68] סימן שח סעיף ג. [69] ארחות שבת פי"ט הערה מא, הלכות מוקצה עמוד 20, שו"ת באר משה ח"א סימן כא, מגילת ספר עמוד רנז, וע"ע נחלת ישראל עמוד קס וחוט שני ח"ג עמוד עז אות ד. [70] נחלת ישראל עמוד קסב. [71] ארחות שבת פי"ט סעיף כא, כג, לה. [72] מ"ב סימן שח ס"ק כד, שש"כ פ"כ הערה לג בשם הגרשז"א. [73] חזו"א סימן מט סק"ח. [74] סימן שח סעיף ג ומ"ב ס"ק יג, ארחות שבת פי"ט הערה נב. [75] שו"ע ומ"ב שם. [76] מ"ב ס"ק טו. [77] מ"ב ס"ק טז, ארחות שבת פי"ט

סעיף יט עם ההערות, וע"ע שבת בשבת פכ"ד סעיף ו.   [78] פרמ"ג א"א סק"ח, גר"ז סעיף יב.   [79] חוט שני עמוד פ ד"ה וכל וד"ה ולהזיז, ארחות שבת פי"ט סעיף כה, טלטולי שבת פסקי הגרמ"פ אות ו, וע"ע מחזה אליהו ח"א סימן מו שמתיר.   [80] ערוה"ש סעיף יד, טלטולי שבת עמוד 40 הערה 14.

פרק ד - מכשירי חשמל

[81] אג"מ ח"ג סימן מט, שש"כ פי"ג סעיף מ, ארחות שבת פי"ט סעיף ה, וע"ע אג"מ ח"ה סימן כג שכ' שאינו מוקצה וצ"ע, וע"ע חוט שני ח"ג עמוד סא לחוש שיש פי לחוש שהוא בסיס לזרם החשמל.   [82] שם, וע"ע מנח"ש סימן ט שאם פועל אינו מוקצה, וכ"כ בפסקי הגרי"ש עמוד קלה אות מא, וע"ע נחלת ישראל עמוד קעב שאם אינו פועל הוי מוקצה מחמת גופו.   [83] ארחות שבת פרק יט סעיף ה.   [84] ארחות שבת שם.   [85] ארחות שבת פי"ט סעיף כב, מבית לוי ח"ו עמוד מז אות ט.   [86] שש"כ פי"ג סעיף מ.   [87] ארחות שבת פי"ט סעיף מט, לוח המוקצה ערך דלת תנור.   [88] פשוט.   [89] ארחות שבת פרק יט סעיף נא, לוח המוקצה ערך דלת - מכונת ייבוש.   [90] שם סעיף נא, לוח המוקצה ערך דלת - מדיח כלים, שש"כ פי"ב סעיף לח, וע"ע מחז"א סימן ס דס"ל שמדיח כלים אינו מוקצה שהדרך להשתמש בו כמו ארון, ועיין נחלת ישראל עמוד קפו שמקשה עליו שעיקרו עומד לאיסור וא"כ לפי המבואר בשאלה 45 נחשב כשמל"א ולא להיתר. ולענין הכנה עיין ספר הלכות שבת (איידר) ח"ד תשובה נ' שהגרמ"פ התיר וע"ע בשש"כ שם מבואר שמותר רק אם רגיל להכניס כלים ישר מהשלחן גם בימות החול.   [91] שש"כ פט"ו סעיף כה, לוח המוקצה ערך דלת - מכונת כביסה, וע"ע ארחות שבת פי"ט סעיף נ שמחלק בין רגיל לאינו רגיל לאחסן בה, ואינו מובן דלכאורה די שראוי לכך וכן עושים הרבה אנשים ואינו תלוי בכל אחד.   [92] שש"כ פ"כ סעיף פ, ספר טלטולי שבת עמוד 50 ותשובת הגרמ"פ שם אות ז.   [93] שש"כ פ"כ סעיף עט ופ"י סעיף יב, יד, הלכות מוקצה עמוד 129, לוח המוקצה ערך דלת מכונת כביסה עם הערה.   [94] שש"כ פ"כ סעיף עט והערות רפו*-רפז בשם הגרשז"א, ארחות שבת פי"ט סעיף רצז והערה תלה, שבות יצחק ח"א עמוד קנא.   [95] לוח המוקצה ערך פלטה חשמלית דולקת/כבויה.   [96] לוח המוקצה ערך פלטה חשמלית דולקת עם הערה, ארחות שבת פי"ט סעיף מא, קפג, וע"ע אז נדברו ח"ג סימן נד אות ח שאין הבדל בין מחובר לאינו מחובר ושניהם כלי שמלאכתו לאיסור.   [97] ארחות שבת פי"ט סעיף מא.   [98] פשוט.   [99] בהלכות מוקצה עמוד 125 כ' שאם הוא מנותק הוי כשמל"א סוג ב' דאין לו שימוש היתר, ובלוח המוקצה ערך רדיאטור כבוי והערה שם כ' שהוא סוג א' דראוי להניח עליו

דברים, ויש לעיין אם אנשים עושים כן, ועיין ארחות שבת פי"ט סעיף קפד והערה רמז. [100] ארחות שבת פי"ט סעיף קפא והערה רמג. [101] לוח המוקצה ערך כבל חשמל עם ההערה, הלכות מוקצה עמוד 128. [102] ספר טלטולי שבת עמוד 20 בשם הגרמ"פ, לוח המוקצה ערך שעון יד, ששכ"ב פכ"ח סעיף כ. [103] ארחות שבת פי"ט סעיף מג. [104] שש"כ פכ"ח סעיף כ. [105] שם סעיף כד, נחלת ישראל עמוד רפב ד"ה גם. [106] שש"כ פכ"ח סעיף לד, ארחות שבת פי"ט סעיף כז, ועיי"ש בהערה מו שיש להמנע מלהשתמש בו כשעון מעורר משום זלזול שבת. [107] שם.

פרק ה - מוקצה מחמת חסרון כיס

[108] סימן שח סעיף א, מ"ב סק"ב. [109] שם. [110] סעיף א. [111] מ"ב סק"ג, חוט שני ח"ג עמוד נז ד"ה ודע. [112] עיין אג"מ ח"ד סימן עב ד"ה ולכן, חוט שני ח"ג עמוד נח ד"ה נייר דס"ל שהוא ממחו"כ. ועיין שש"כ פ"כ הערה נו, לוח המוקצה ערך דף נייר חלק עם ההערה דס"ל שהוא כשמל"א. ועיין מבית לוי ח"ו עמוד מו אות ג, פסקי הגרי"ש או"ח עמוד קכט אות ב, מכתבי הגרשז"א בספר מאור השבת ח"א עמוד תצח דס"ל שאינו מוקצה "שאין מקפידים לנגב את הידיים או שאר לכלוך עם נייר העומד לכתיבה". [113] דינים והנהגות להחזו"א פי"ד אות כא, תשובת הגרמ"פ בספר טלטולי שבת אות יז, ועיין שש"כ פ"כ סעיף פז והערה שיא בשם הגרשז"א. [114] תשובת הגרמ"פ שם, ועיין מכתבי הגרשז"א בספר מאור השבת ח"ב עמוד תקנו דס"ל שקלסר דינו כמחברת. [115] לוח המוקצה ערך מעטפות שסגירתן בלא דבק, נחלת ישראל עמוד רלו הערה יח, וע"ע הלכות מוקצה עמוד 176 שכתב שהוא מוקצה מחמת חסרון כיס. [116] נחלת ישראל עמוד רלג. [117] הלכות מוקצה עמוד 179-180, ארחות שבת פי"ט סעיף צה, צז. [118] הלכות מוקצה עמוד 188, שלמי יהודה פי"ב סעיף יג בשם הגריש"א, שש"כ פ"כ הערה נט בשם הגרשז"א, וע"ע ארחות שבת פכ"ב הערה רח ולוח המוקצה ערך כתובה שמחלקים בין כתובה לגט. [119] ארחות שבת פי"ט סעיף צד, שש"כ פ"כ סעיף כ, כג, לוח המוקצה ערך בול. [120] ארחות שבת פי"ט סעיף קג, שש"כ פ"כ סעיף כב, פסקי הגרי"ש עמוד קל אות ח. [121] ארחות שבת פי"ט הערה קלא, לוח המוקצה ערך שעון קיר עם ההערה. [122] הלכות מוקצה עמוד 55, שש"כ פ"כ סעיף כד. [123] שש"כ פ"כ סעיף כב. [124] עיין חזו"א סימן מג אות יז שכל שקובע לה מקום ה"ז ממחו"כ, ועיין תשובת הגרמ"פ בספר טלטולי שבת אות יג שכיון שתלוה שם לנוי אינה מוקצה. [125] מ"ב סק"ח, פסקי הגרי"ש עמוד קכט אות ו, ארחות שבת פי"ט סעיף קד, ספר טלטולי שבת עמוד 67. [126] עיין חוט שני ח"ג עמוד פח, מבית לוי ח"ו עמוד מו אות ב, אז נדברו ח"ט סימן כד דס"ל שאינן ממחו"כ,

ובשש"כ פ"כ הערה עז בשם הגרשז"א כ' שאפשר שאינו מוקצה, ועיין פסקי הגרי"ש עמוד קל אות ז, שש"כ שם סעיף כב דס"ל שהם ממחה"כ כיון שמקפיד עליהם.   [127] חוט שני ח"ג עמוד פח, לוח המוקצה הערה 345, נחלת ישראל עמוד תרפב בשם הגרח"ק.
[128] סימן שח סעיף א ברמ"א, מ"ב ס"ק ו-ז.   [129] סימן שי סעיף ב, מ"ב סק"ד, חיי"א כלל סו סימן ב, וע"ע ארחות שבת פי"ט הערה קלח.   [130] שש"כ פ"כ סעיף כא בשם הגרשז"א.   [131] ארחות שבת פי"ט סעיף צט, חוט שני ח"ג עמוד ע ד"ה ודע.   [132] שו"ת באר משה ח"ח סימן עב, פסקי הגרי"ש עמוד קלא אות יג.   [133] שבה"ל ח"ד סימן קמג, צי"א חי"ג סימן נג.   [134] שם, ועיין ארחות שבת פ"ח סעיף כג, כד, שש"כ פכ"ג הערה קיז.   [135] תשובת הגרשז"א בספר טלטולי שבת אות ו, חוט שני עמוד ע ד"ה הקונה, לוח המוקצה ערך בגד חדש שדעתו להחזירו.   [136] לוח המוקצה ערך מתנה שדעתו ליתנו בשבת/לאחר שבת.   [137] שם ערך מציאה.

פרק ו - מוקצה מחמת גופו

[138] הקדמת המ"ב לסימן שח חלק ב, גר"ז סעיף ט, סימן תרלח סעיף ב.   [139] סימן שח סעיף ז ורמ"א.   [140] הקדמת המ"ב שם.   [141] שם, ארחות שבת פי"ט, סעיף ז, קכה, קכו, קל, לוח המוקצה.   [142] זכור ושמור עמוד 9, לוח המוקצה ערך נפט עם הערה.   [143] לוח המוקצה ערך מטבעות כסף עם הערה.   [144] סימן שח סעיף כא, כב.   [145] מ"ב סימן רעט סק"א ושעה"צ סק"ד, סימן שח ס"ק לד, ועיין ארחות שבת פי"ט הערה כה, שש"כ פי"ד הערה קד, ספר טלטולי שבת עמוד 82, ובלוח המוקצה ערך נר שעוה כ' לבאר דהוי כמל"א משום שיש לו היתר שימוש בשבת אם מדליקו מבעוד יום.   [146] ספר טלטולי שבת עמוד 81 והערה 17, 18 בשם הגרמ"פ, ועיין שלמי יהודה בשם הגריש"א פ"ג הערה עד*, ועיין לוח המוקצה ערך גפרור, וע"ע שש"כ פ"כ הערה מ.   [147] תשובת הגרמ"פ בספר טלטולי שבת אות טו, שלמי יהודה פרק ט סעיף ג בשם הגריש"א, חוט שני ח"ג עמוד פב, ועיין לוח המוקצה ערך סבון, וע"ע הלכות מוקצה עמוד 98, ארחות שבת פי"ט הערה כד, פי"ז סעיף כז.   [148] סימן שלו סעיף ב, יג, מ"ב סימן שח ס"ק פא.   [149] סימן שלו סעיף ב, מ"ב ס"ק יט.   [150] שם וס"ק יד, כד, שש"כ פכ"ו סעיף כ, לוח המוקצה ערך דשא לישיבה, וכן שמעננו מהגרצ"ו, וע"ע הלכות מוקצה עמוד 231 ושבות יצחק ח"א עמוד צח.   [151] סימן שלו סעיף י, מ"ב ס"ק מח, סימן רטז סעיף ב.   [152] הדין שונה בעציץ נקוב לאינו נקוב, ובפנים ובחוץ, וסוג הצמח, ואם קבע לו מקום, לכן כדי למנוע מטעויות עדיף להחמיר בכולם. ועיין בארחות שבת פי"ט סעיף קמא, שש"כ פכ"ו סעיף ב.   [153] ארחות שבת פי"ט סעיף קמג-קמד, שש"כ פכ"ו סעיף כה, כו.

[154] ספר טלטולי שבת עמוד 31. [155] פשוט. [156] פשוט.
[157] סימן שח סעיף כט, מ"ב ס"ק קכז. [158] סעיף כט. [159]
סעיף לא, מ"ב ס"ק קכה, ערוה"ש סעיף נח, ארחות שבת פי"ט
הערה קנז. [160] נחלת ישראל עמוד תקלח. [161] סימן שי סעיף
ב, ערוה"ש סימן שח סעיף נח, ארחות שבת פי"ט סעיף קכ, שש"כ
פל"ד הערה יח, וע"ע לוח המוקצה ערך ביצים חיות. [162] ספר
טלטולי שבת עמוד 104, ארחות שבת פי"ט הערה קס, שלמי יהודה
פ"ח הערה כו בשם הגריש"א. [163] ספר טלטולי שבת שם, לוח
המוקצה ערך תה. [164] ספר טלטולי שבת עמוד 106, הלכות
מוקצה עמוד 5 הערה 8, שבת בשבת ח"ב עמוד עדר הערה 27,
וע"ע ארחות שבת פי"ט הערה תקמז. [165] עיין לוח המוקצה
ערך פותחן שימורים עם הערה. [166] שם. [167] הלכות
מוקצה עמוד 198, ועיין מ"ב סימן שיד ס"ק יז. [168] ארחות שבת
פי"ט סעיף קכב. [169] ארחות שבת פי"ט סעיף קיז, שע, נחלת
ישראל עמוד שטו, וע"ע פסקי הגרי"ש עמוד קלה אות מו שצריך
שיהיה דעתו עליו שיגמר בשבת. [170] נחלת ישראל עמוד ריט,
רכ. [171] סעיף כט. [172] ארחות שבת פי"ט הערה קצו, לוח
המוקצה ערך פירורי לחם שדרך לאוכלם בסעודה, חוט שני ח"ג
עמוד קכה. [173] חוט שני שם. [174] מנחת שבת סימן פח ס"ק
טז, שש"כ פ"כ סעיף לז, תשובת הגרמ"פ בספר טלטולי שבת אות
כג. [175] שש"כ שם, ארחות שבת פי"ט סעיף קכז, לוח המוקצה
ערך תרופות לחולה שחלה מבעוד יום ותרופות שתשמישן מצוי,
ועיין תשובת הגרמ"פ הנ"ל. [176] שם, ערוה"ש סימן שח סעיף
נט. [177] שש"כ פ"כ הערה קמב, ארחות שבת פי"ט סעיף קכט,
חוט שני ח"ג עמוד סד ד"ה בתי. [178] ע"פ הנ"ל. [179] מ"ב סימן
שכח ס"ק נח, שש"כ פל"ג הערה לב. [180] חוט שני ח"ג עמוד סד
ד"ה ולעניננו וד"ה ומ"מ, עמוד קח אות ג. [181] מ"ב סימן שכח ס"ק
קכ, שש"כ פל"ד סעיף כ והערה פו, ארחות שבת פ"כ סעיף קלח,
לוח המוקצה ערך ויטמנים. [182] שש"כ פל"ז סעיף ב, ד, וע"ע
לוח המוקצה ערך ויטמנים מתוקים לילדים והערה שם, ואינו מובן.
[183] עיין שש"כ פל"ג סעיף טז והערה עד, חוט שני ח"ד עמוד קנב
אות ב, ארחות שבת פ"כ הערה רד. [184] פשוט. [185] אג"מ
או"ח ח"א סימן קכח, מנח"י ח"ג סימן קמב. [186] זכור ושמור
ממחק עמוד 17, אז נדברו ח"ג סו"ס כא, ארחות שבת פ"ח סעיף
לד. [187] שש"כ פל"ה סעיף כז, הלכות מוקצה עמוד 207. [188]
סימן שח סעיף ו, רמ"א, מ"ב ס"ק כח. [189] שם, מ"ב ס"ק כז.
[190] פשוט. [191] סעיף ו. [192] מ"ב ס"ק לב. [193] שם.
[194] ארחות שבת פי"ט סעיף קנח, שש"כ פ"כ סעיף מב, ספר
טלטולי שבת עמוד 88 הערה 42 בשם הגרמ"פ, וע"ע חוט שני ח"ג
עמוד קה. [195] נחלת ישראל עמוד שט, ועיי"ש מה דינו אם יש

בו משקה. [196] לוח המוקצה. [197] מ"ב סימן שח ס"ק קיד, לוח המוקצה ערך עצמות מבושלות שיש עליהם בשר והערה שם, נחלת ישראל עמוד קעט וע"ע שש"כ פ"כ סעיף כו. [198] חוט שני ח"ג עמוד קכה ד"ה וה"ה, לוח המוקצה ערך עצמות מבושלות שיש בהם מוח. [199] עיין שאלה 197. [200] עיין ביה"ל סעיף ל סד"ה גרעיני, ועיין לוח המוקצה ערך גרעין שזיף והערה שם בשם הגר"צ ובר שהיום נשתנה הדין. [201] לוח המוקצה. [202] עיין ביה"ל הנ"ל שמסתפק, ועיין חוט שני ח"ג עמוד קלג ולוח המוקצה ערך גרעין פתוח בשם הגרצ"ו שמחמירין, ועיין ארחות שבת פי"ט הערה קצח. [203] חוט שני ח"ג עמוד קלג, שבות יצחק ח"א עמוד פא בשם הגריש"א, וע"ע שש"כ פט"ז הערה לג. [204] גר"ז סימן שח סעיף סז, ערוה"ש סעיף נא, שבות יצחק ח"א עמוד קטז, ארחות שבת פי"ט סעיף קנד, וע"ע שש"כ פ"כ סעיף כו. [205] לוח המוקצה, הלכות מוקצה עמוד 165-162. [206] לוח המוקצה, הלכות מוקצה שם. [207] עיין שאלה 197. [208] סימן שח סעיף כז, כט. [209] עיין שאלה 505. [210] נחלת ישראל עמוד שג, ועמוד שלח בשם הגרפ"א פאלק, לוח המוקצה ערך גביע גבינה ריק עם ההערה. [211] ארחות שבת פי"ט סעיף קסב, לוח המוקצה ערך כוס חד פעמי משומש. [212] עיין חוט שני ח"ג עמוד קו שמחלק בין זרקו מבע"י לזרקו בשבת, וכ"כ בארחות שבת פי"ט הערות ריא, ריג, ועיין שלחן שלמה סימן שח ס"ק לו שמחמיר אפילו זרקו בשבת וכ"כ בשלמי יהונתן ח"ג בירורי הלכות סימן לז בשם הגריש"א וכ"כ בלוח המוקצה ערך כוס חד פעמי משומש שזרק לאשפה. [213] עיין מאור השבת ח"ב עמוד תקסג בשם הגרשז"א שהם מוקצה מיד כיון שעומדים לזרוק, ועיין מקורות הנ"ל לענין אם זרקו מבע"י או בשבת. [214] עיין פסקי הגרי"ש או"ח עמוד קלו מח שהם מוקצה מיד, וכ"כ בנחלת ישראל עמוד שלח בשם מחז"א, וכן ד' הגרשז"א הנ"ל. [215] ארחות שבת פי"ט סעיף שנח. [216] שם הערה תקל, ועו' י"ל דהוי גרף. [217] ביה"ל סימן שלח סעיף ח ד"ה אסור. [218] סימן שח סעיף לט, מ"ב ס"ק קמו. [219] גר"ז סעיף עח, דעת תורה סעיף לט, תשובת הגרמ"פ בספר טלטולי שבת אות כד, ועיין שש"כ פכ"ז הערה קא. [220] פשוט. [221] עיין ביה"ל סימן שב סעיף יא ד"ה מקנחה, שש"כ פכ"ז הערה נו. [222] עיין דיני טלטול מן הצד, ועיין סימן שח סעיף מג. [223] עיין שש"כ פי"ח הערה סב בשם הגרשז"א שנוטה להתיר, אג"מ או"ח ח"א סימן מה ד"ה וכן כיון, ועיין לוח המוקצה ערך בע"ח המסייע לעור שמחמיר, וכן נוטה בנחלת ישראל עמוד רט. [224] שש"כ פכ"ז סעיף לא והערה קח, כה"ח סימן שי ס"ק לח, טלטולי שבת עמוד 121. [225] טלטולי

שבת עמוד 121, ארחות שבת פי"ט סעיף קכד והערה קסח, שש"כ פכ"ז סעיף כז והערה קא. [226] תהל"ד סימן שכח ס"ק עט.

פרק ז - יחוד

[227] סימן שח סעיף כב. [228] סימן שי סעיף ג. [229] מ"ב סימן שח ס"ק צב. [230] פשוט. [231] סעיף כב. [232] מ"ב ס"ק צג. [233] חזו"א סימן מג סוף ס"ק יג. [234] מ"ב ס"ק צד. [235] מ"ב ס"ק צז. [236] פשוט. [237] פשוט. [238] עיין סעיף כ ומ"ב ס"ק פג דשימוש פ"א מועיל אם דרכו בכך, ובס"ק כ' דרגיל להשתמש מועיל אם אין דרכו בכך, ועיין חזו"א סימן מב סוסק"ט דלא מהני שימוש אם אין דרכו בכך. [239] מ"ב ס"ק מח. [240] פרמ"ג א"א ס"ק עב, פתיחה כוללת הלכות יום טוב חלק השני פרק הראשון אות ו, שש"כ פט"ז הערה לא, נחלת ישראל עמוד תקכג. [241] ערוה"ש סעיף מז, ועיין שש"כ פ"ך הערה פא. [242] סימן שח סעיף כו, סימן רנט סעיף א ומ"ב סק"ה, שש"כ פ"ה סעיף כג. [243] תשובת הגרשז"א בספר טלטולי שבת אות ב, חזו"א סימן מג סק"א.

פרק ח - מוקצה מחמת איסור

[244] גר"ז סימן שח סעיף ט, פ"ה, שו"ע סימן שח סעיף טז ומ"ב ס"ק סח, רמ"א סימן שא סעיף מו. [245] גר"ז סימן שח סעיף ט. [246] טבל, בשר בחלב, יין נסך - גר"ז שם. חמץ - סימן תמו מ"ב סק"ה. שעטנז - סימן שח סעיף מז ומ"ב ס"ק קסא. [247] גר"ז שם, שעה"צ סימן תקו סק"ל. [248] סימן שלט סעיף ד, מ"ב ס"ק כה-כו, רמב"ם הלכות מעשר פי"ג הט"ו, פרמ"ג מ"ז סו"ס שח, ועיין שש"כ פ"כ הערה קו. [249] ארחות שבת פכ"ב הערה קיא. [250] מ"ב סימן שלט ס"ק כה. [251] נחלת ישראל עמוד רלט ע"פ פרמ"ג סימן שלח א"א סק"ג, ארחות שבת פכ"ב סעיף עה. [252] שש"כ פ"כ סעיף ל. [253] גר"ז סימן תנז סעיף ו, רמ"א סימן תקו סעיף ג. [254] פשוט. [255] יו"ד סימן פז סעיף א, גר"ז סימן שח סעיף ט. [256] יו"ד שם סעיף ג, סימן צא סעיף ח, גר"ז שם. [257] גר"ז שם. [258] רמב"ם הלכות עבודה זרה פרק ז הלכה טו, גר"ז שם. [259] יו"ד סימן קכג סעיף א ורמ"א, ספר טלטולי שבת עמוד 131. [260] רמ"א סימן תמו סעיף א, מ"ב סק"ה, סעיף ג ורמ"א. [261] שם. [262] סימן תמג סעיף א, מ"ב סימן תמד ס"ק כא. [263] מ"ב סימן תנג ס"ק יב, ארחות שבת פי"ט סעיף ריד, שש"כ פ"כ סעיף לד, וע"ע משנת הגרי"ש (פסח) פרק ח סעיף ט שאוסר. [264] גר"ז סימן שח סעיף ט, שש"כ פ"כ הערה קכה. [265] רמ"א סו"ס תריב, ארחות שבת פי"ט סעיף קלז. [266] עיין שלמי יהודה פ"ד הערה טו* בשם הגרי"ש"א דהוו כלים שמלאכתם לאיסור, ועיי"ש בקונטרס בענייני מוקצה שם סימן טו בשם הגרחפ"ש להקל, וכן שמעונו מאת הגר"ח וכן בחוט שני הלכות ר"ה ויו"כ עמוד קלז אות א,

ועיין הליכות שלמה מועדים ח"ב סימן ה סעיף כא שנוטה להקל, וע"ע שלמי יהונתן ח"ג בירורי הלכות סימן מ. [267] שו"ע סימן שח סעיף מז, מ"ב ס"ק קסא, ועיין בלכלכת שבת מוקצה אות ב' שאם דעתנו ליתנו לגוי אינו מוקצה אבל עיין שש"כ פ"כ הערה קמג בשם הגרשז"א שאם השעטנז ניכר אסור ליתנו לגוי. [268] שבת בשבת ח"ב פ"כ סעיף כב והערה 35 בשם הגריש"א. [269] סימן יד סעיף ג, שבה"ל ח"ג סימן לא. [270] סימן שכג סעיף ז, ועיין ספר טלטולי שבת עמוד 134 שאפשר להשתמש בו לדברים אחרים, ועיין נחלת ישראל עמוד רמו הערה יד דזה לא מהני שאינו עומד לזה. [271] ערה"ש סימן שט סעיף א, ספר טלטולי שבת עמוד 134, ועיין שלמי יהודה פ"ו הערה לה. [272] סימן שח סעיף טז ומ"ב ס"ק סח, רמ"א סימן שא סעיף מו, סימן שכ"ג סעיף ג, סימן שכ סעיף א. [273] סימן שח סעיף טז, רמ"א. [274] רמ"א, מ"ב ס"ק עא. [275] מ"ב ס"ק סט, ארחות שבת פי"ט סעיף קע אות א. [276] נחלת ישראל עמוד רסח בשם הגרח"ק. [277] סימן שח סעיף ח, ארחות שבת הערה ריז, שלחן שלמה אות מה, זכור ושמור מכה בפטיש עמוד 13. [278] עיין מ"ב סימן שח ס"ק לה שחלק שהתפרק אינו מוקצה אפילו אם אינו ראוי לשימוש כיון שעומד להתחבר, וכן פסקו בארחות שבת פי"ט סעיף קסו, זכור ושמור מוקצה עמוד 60, אז נדברו ח"ז סימן מו, אבל עיין ערוה"ש סעיף כה שדוקא אם ראוי לשימוש, וכן פסק הגרמ"פ בספר טלטולי שבת אות יח, ועיין שש"כ פ"כ סעיף עב בשם הגרשז"א שטוב להחמיר. [279] פסקי תוס' הרי"ד שבת קכב/ב הובא לדינא בחוט שני ח"ג עמוד קיג ד"ה מבואר, אז נדברו ח"ז סימן מו, שלמי יהונתן פ"ג הערה טו בשם הגרשז"א. [280] מ"ב ס"ק לה, ארחות שבת פי"ט הערה רלו. [281] ארחות שבת פי"ט סעיף קעו, קעח. [282] פסקי הגרי"ש עמוד קלט אות עג, ועיין חוט שני ח"ב עמוד רנא ד"ה וה"ה. [283] עיין חוט שני עמוד קיט, טלטולי שבת עמוד 147, לוח המוקצה ערך עגלה שנפל גלגל שמחמירים שעגלה דינה כמו כירה שנשמטה א' מרגליה. ועיין נחלת ישראל עמוד רפא בשם הגרשז"א והגריש"א שמקילים שעגלה בלי רגל א' יותר שימושי מכירה שנשמטה א' מרגליה וגם יש לה כמה השתמשויות ולכן אינה דומה לכירה אלא לשידה בלי דלת, וכן מבואר דעת הגרשז"א בזה בשש"כ פכ"ד הערה נג. [284] פשוט. [285] מ"ב סימן שח ס"ק עב. [286] פשוט ע"פ הנ"ל. [287] עיין ארחות שבת סעיף קעא, חוט שני עמוד קיט, פסקי הגרי"ש עמוד קלח אות סט שמחמירין, ועיין טלטולי שבת עמוד 147 בשם הגרמ"פ ואז נדברו ח"ח סימן לג אות ד שמקילין. [288] מאור השבת ח"ב עמוד תר בשם הגרשז"א, זכור ושמור מכה בפטיש עמוד 13, וע"ע חוט שני ח"ב עמוד רנא אות יד. [289] שש"כ פט"ו סעיף פב, ונראה שכאן לכו"ע דמי לרגל

שלחן שאין אדם לובש משקפיים עם עדשה אחת, וכ"כ בהלכות מוקצה עמוד 114 הערה 23. [290] פשוט, ועיין שש"כ פכ"ח סעיף כד כעין זה לענין שעון שנעמד. [291] עיין שאלה 278 לענין חלק שהתפרק ואינו ראוי לשימוש, ועיין נחלת ישראל עמוד רעד, ארחות שבת פי"ט סעיף קסז, שש"כ פט"ו סעיף עב והערה רלד, הגרמ"פ בספר טלטולי שבת אות יח. [292] עיין ארחות שבת פי"ט סעיף קעג שמחמיר, ועיין חוט שני ח"ג עמוד קכא ד"ה מטאטא שמקיל. [293] סימן שא סעיף מה, רמ"א סעיף מו, מ"ב ס"ק קעא, וסימן שיט ס"ק לט. [294] מ"ב סימן שח ס"ק סג, סימן פב סק"ג, סימן שב ס"ק לט אות ב. [295] שש"כ פט"ו הערה נ בשם הגרשז"א. [296] זכור ושמור מלבן עמוד 17, מ"ב סימן שיט ס"ק לח-לט ושעה"צ ס"ק כט. [297] סימן שא סעיף מה, מ"ב ס"ק קסב. [298] גר"ז סעיף נו, שש"כ פט"ו הערה נח. [299] עיין שעה"צ סימן שא ס"ק ריב. [300] מ"ב ס"ק קסב. [301] נחלת ישראל עמוד רסט, זכור ושמור מלבן עמוד 21. [302] עיין מ"ב סימן שא ס"ק קעה ושעה"צ ס"ק ריד שנחלקו הפוסקים אם אדם מקפיד על מגבת רטובה, ועיין הלכות שבת במטבח (רש"ב כהן) עמוד 195 הערה 11 בשם הגרחפ"ש שבזה"ז אין מקפידים, וע"ע נחלת ישראל עמוד רסח. [303] מ"ב ס"ק קעב. [304] סימן שכ סעיף יז, מ"ב ס"ק מח, בה"ל שם, ארחות שבת פי"ט סעיף פג והערה קד. [305] זכור ושמור מלבן עמוד 16. [306] א"ר סימן שא סוף סק"פ, נחלת ישראל עמוד ערב, זכור ושמור מלבן עמוד 20, ועיין שש"כ פט"ו הערה נה. [307] פשוט, עיין שאלה 296. [308] ארחות שבת פי"ט סעיף עג, ועיין זכור ושמור החדש עמוד 225 ביאור הענין באריכות, ושבה"ל ח"ח סימן נט. [309] מ"ב סימן שכב ס"ק ז. [310] מ"ב סק"ה, שעה"צ סק"ח. [311] מ"ב סימן שי ס"ק יב, וסימן שכה ס"ק כב. [312] סימן שכ סעיף א, וע"ע שבת בשבת פי"א סעיף טו, כח וסוף הערה 23 בשם הגריש"א שפירות הדר דינם כענבים, ועיין חוט שני ח"ב עמוד נה ד"ה מסתפק. [313] מ"ב סק"ו, ארחות שבת פ"ד סעיף כח, כט. [314] מ"ב סק"ד. [315] שש"כ פ"ה סעיף יא, ארחות שבת פ"ד סעיף כט. [316] סימן שכ מ"ב ס"ק כב.

פרק ט - מוקצה מחמת מצוה

[317] סימן תרלח סעיף ב. [318] שם, רמ"א שם. [319] שם, סעיף א, רמ"א סימן תרנח סעיף ב, מ"ב סק"ג. [320] מ"ב סימן תרלח ס"ק כא. [321] סעיף א, מ"ב סק"ב. [322] סימן תרלח סעיף ב ברמ"א ומ"ב ס"ק כד, חוט שני סוכות עמוד רלג אות ב, וע"ע שמחת ישראל סוכות ח"א פרק יז הערה 919 בעניין לנגב ידייהם עליהם. [323] שם אות א, שמחת ישראל שם אות יט. [324] סעיף ב, מ"ב ס"ק יג, בה"ל ד"ה ובייו"ט. [325] נחלקו הפוסקים בכתבי הקודש שהם מוקצה ומוטלים בבזיון האם מותר לטלטלם בלי שינוי לכן

עדיף לטלטלם בשינוי, עיין ששכ"כ פ"כ הערה לג.   [326] מ"ב ס"ק יב-יג.   [327] לוח המוקצה, ארחות שבת פ"ט הערה מח.   [328] סעיף ב, מ"ב ס"ק יג, בה"ל ד"ה וביו"ט.   [329] מ"ב סימן תרל"ז סק"ה, שבת בשבת ח"ב פי"ז סעיף כד והערה שם, ועיין ששכ"כ פכ"ד הערה קלד.   [330] לענין הלולב וערבות עיין רמ"א סימן תרנ"ח סעיף ב ומ"ב סק"ג, לענין הדסים בסוכות עיי"ש ושעה"צ סק"ב, ובשאר שבתות השנה עיין סימן תרנ"ג סעיף ב ומ"ב סק"ד,   [331] סימן תרס"ה סעיף א, ובה"ל ד"ה אתרוג.   [332] סימן רט"ז סעיף ב.   [333] סימן תרנ"ג סעיף א, מ"ב סק"א.   [334] שם, סימן רט"ז סעיף ב, מ"ב סק"ח וסעיף יד וביה"ל שם, וע"ע הליכות שלמה תפלה פכ"ג סעיף לז.   [335] רמ"א סימן תקפ"ח סעיף ה, ועיין מ"ב ס"ק טו שראוי לשאוב בו מים, ובזה"ז אין עושין כן כמבואר בששכ"כ פכ"ח הערה פב בשם הגרשז"א, ועיין פרמ"ג סימן שה א"א ס"ק יב.

פרק י - נולד

[336] סימן שכ"ב סעיף א, מ"ב סימן תצ"ה ס"ק יז.   [337] חיי אדם כלל סו סימן ו.   [338] חיי"א כלל סה סימן ג פן ח, וע"ע ערוה"ש סימן שח סעיף ו, ששכ"כ פי"ג סעיף לט. ועיין גר"ז סימן שה סעיף לב שחלב שנחלב מיד בכניסת השבת אין לו דין נולד גמור.   [339] ששכ"כ פל"ו סעיף כא.   [340] פשוט, וכ"כ בנחלת ישראל עמוד שא בהערה ד"ה ופשוט.   [341] מ"ב סימן שלח סק"ל.   [342] עיין ארחות שבת פי"ט-הערה רנ"ט בשם הגרישו"א, ששכ"כ פט"ז הערה קי"ח בשם הגרשז"א, מחז"א ח"א סימן סח שמקילים. וע"ע אג"מ או"ח ח"ה סימן כב אות לז שמחמיר.   [343] מ"ב סימן תצ"ה ס"ק יז, סימן תק"א ס"ק כב, כח.   [344] סימן שח סעיף כט.   [345] מ"ב סימן תק"א ס"ק כב, טלטולי שבת עמוד 89.   [346] מ"ב סימן תק"א ס"ק כח, שעה"צ ס"ק לה, טלטולי שבת עמוד 171.   [347] לענין שבת עיין סימן שכ"ב סעיף ט, רמ"א סימן שיח סעיף טז, מ"ב ס"ק קז, לענין יו"ט עיין ששכ"כ פי"ב הערה לא בשם הגרשז"א, ופ"י סעיף ז, לקט הלכות יו"ט (הגרי"י דינר) פי"ד סעיף ז בשם הגריש"א, ושבה"ל.

פרק יא - בסיס

[348] סימן ש"י סעיף ז, ועיין רש"י שבת מז/א ד"ה הא ליכא.   [349] מ"ב סימן רנ"ט סק"ט.   [350] דין א' פשוט. דין ב' וג' עיין ארחות שבת פי"ט הערה תכ"ח, ששכ"כ פ"כ הערה קע"ט, טלטולי שבת עמוד 175 הערה 3, וע"ע שבת בשבת פכ"ה סעיף יט והערה 38.   [351] מ"ב סימן ש"י ס"ק כד, ארחות שבת פי"ט הערה שפ"ד, וכ"כ ששכ"כ פ"כ סעיף נ.   [352] רמ"א סימן ש"י סעיף ז ומ"ב ס"ק כד, ארחות שבת פי"ט סעיף רע"ח.   [353] רמ"א סימן ש"ט סעיף ד.   [354] אג"מ או"ח ח"ג סימן נ"א, ועיין טלטולי שבת עמוד 185 הערה 22 שלא נעשו בסיס זה לזה אלא כולם נעשו בסיס למוקצה שלמעלה.   [355] ששכ"כ פ"כ סעיף סב, ועיין ארחות שבת פי"ט סעיף רצ, נחלת

ישראל עמוד תט, מ״ב סימן שט ס״ק יח, שעה״צ ס״ק כד, אג״מ ח״ד סימן עג. [357] סימן שט סעיף ד, מ״ב ס״ק יח, ועיין מ״ב סימן שט ס״ק כא שיש להקל במקום הפסד. [358] מ״ב סימן שט ס״ק כא, ועיי״ש שיש להקל במקום הפסד. [359] עיין מ״ב סימן שט ס״ק כא ושעה״צ סק״ב שלא הכריע בדין הג, ועיין שבת בשבת פכ״ה סעיף ג, ועיין שלמי יהונתן הלכות מוקצה פ״ו סעיף ב. [360] אג״מ או״ח ח״ג סימן נא, שבות יצחק ח״א סוף פט״ו בשם הגרי״שא, חוט שני ח״ג עמוד קנה אות ד, וע״ע שש״כ פ״כ הערה רכח. [361] מ״ב סימן שט ס״ק יח. [362] טלטולי שבת עמוד 179. [363] מ״ב סימן שט ס״ק יט, גר״ז סימן שי סעיף ז. [364] שבות יצחק ח״א עמוד קפב בשם הגרי״שא. [365] שם. [366] שם עמוד קפא, נחלת ישראל עמוד תלא, ומ״ש במ״ב סימן רעג ס״ק יח קודם הדלקת הנרות לאו דוקא. [367] נחלת ישראל עמוד תל. [368] פרמ״ג א״א סו״ס רעט. [369] נחלקו הראשונים בדין זה והמ״ב לכ׳ סותר א״ע, עיין ארחות שבת פי״ט הערה תז, טלטולי שבת עמוד 181 הערה 12, נחלת ישראל עמוד תלד, הלכות שבת בשבת פכ״ה סעיף יב והערה 23 בשם הגרי״שא. [370] סימן שי סעיף ג, בה״ל סעיף ז ד״ה והניחם, ארחות שבת פי״ט סעיף רפג. [371] עיין שבות יצחק ח״א עמוד ר. [372] כנ״ל. [373] ארחות שבת פי״ט סעיף רפג, נחלת ישראל עמוד תלה. [374] ארחות שבת פי״ט סעיף רפד, שבות יצחק ח״א עמוד רג. [375] שם. [376] פשוט. [377] רמ״א סימן שט סעיף ד, מ״ב ס״ק כז. [378] מ״ב ס״ק כה. [379] נחלת ישראל עמוד תטז, ארחות שבת פי״ט הערה שצה ד״ה ולענין אורח. [380] ארחות שבת שם ד״ה עיין, שבת בשבת פכ״ה סעיף ה והערה 10 בשם הגרי״שא, חוט שני ח״א עמוד קנה אות ו. [381] מנחת שבת סימן פח סעיף סג הובא בנחלת ישראל עמוד תיז ושש״כ פ״כ הערה קצט, וע״ע ארחות שבת הנ״ל ד״ה ולענין קטן, פסק״ת סימן שט הערה 87. [382] ארחות שבת שם ד״ה יל״ע בשם מהרש״ם, אז נדברו ח״י סוף סימן ג (א). [383] ארחות שבת שם ד״ה ולענין בחורים, חוט שני ח״ג עמוד קנו אות ט, מבית לוי ח״ח עמוד כב. [384] מ״ב סימן שי ס״ק לא. [385] ספר טלטולי שבת עמוד 197. [386] ארחות שבת פי״ט סעיף רצה, נחלת ישראל עמוד תלח ד״ה מוקצה. [387] תהל״ד סימן שי סק״ז, נחלת ישראל עמוד תנח, וע״ע ארחות שבת פי״ט סעיף שיד ושמב שכ׳ שהוא כשמל״א, וע״ע חוט שני ח״ג עמוד קס אות ב שכ׳ שאם הוא מחובר הוי בסיס, ודבריהם אינם מובנים. [388] ארחות שבת פי״ט הערה תקי, נחלת ישראל עמוד תנד. [389] לוח המוקצה ערך פח אשפה ריק, פח אשפה עם אשפה, משולש כיור עם הההערות. [390] ארחות שבת פי״ט סעיף רצט. ויש לעיין למה מועיל הנחת דבר שאינו מוקצה בתוך המגירה, שלכאורה הוי טלטול מן הצד לפח

לצורך דבר האסור שזה אסור, ועיין נחלת ישראל עמוד תמט הערה נט שכ' דנחשב לצורך כבוד שבת שמותר. [391] עיין הלכות מוקצה עמוד 201 והערה 20 שמחמיר, ועיין נחלת ישראל הנ"ל שנוטה להקל, ועיין ארחות שבת פי"ט סעיף רחצ שמסתפק, ועיין ששכ"כ פ"ע סעיף עז. [392] ארחות שבת פי"ט סעיף שמז, שש"כ פכ"ג סעיף יג. [393] ארחות שבת פי"ט סעיף רפב. [394] סימן שי סעיף ח. [395] שם. [396] חיי"א כלל סז סימן ד, מ"ב סימן רעז ס"ק יח, הלכות מוקצה עמוד 67, זכור ושמור עמוד 29. [397] נחלת ישראל עמוד תכב. [398] עיין פרמ"ג סימן רעט א"א ס"ק יד אות ג שמסתפק, ועיין שבות יצחק ח"א עמוד קצו בשם הגריש"א שהחמיר, וכן מביא לוי ח"ו עמוד מח אות טו, וכן תשובת הגרמ"פ בספר טלטולי שבת אות ל, וע"ע תשובת הגרשז"א שם אות טו שמקיל. [399] סימן רעז סעיף א, מ"ב סק"ז, שבות יצחק ח"א עמוד קנג בשם הגריש"א. [400] סימן שט סעיף ד. [401] שם. [402] שם, סעיף ה, מ"ב ס"ק טז, שעה"צ ס"ק יז. [403] פשוט. [404] סעיף ה, מ"ב ס"ק כט. [405] מ"ב ס"ק טז. [406] שעה"צ ס"ק יז, חיי"א כלל סז סימן ב.

פרק יב - כיסים ומגירות

[407] מ"ב סימן שי ס"ק כט, שש"כ פ"כ סעיף עה. [408] ארחות שבת פי"ט סעיף שג. [409] רמ"א סימן שי סעיף ז, ופירש בנחלת ישראל עמוד תמב שחששו טפי כיון שמסיח דעתו מן המוקצה, ומ"ש בארחות שבת שם שמותר ללבשר צ"ע, ועיין שש"כ פכ"ב סעיף מ שמתיר ללובשו שמקום שיש עירוב. [410] מ"ב ס"ק כט. [411] מ"ב סק"ל. [412] שם. [413] פשוט. [414] מ"ב ס"ק כט. [415] שם. [416] שש"כ פ"כ סעיף עה. [417] שם ופי"ח סעיף נט. [418] מ"ב סימן שי ס"ק לא. [419] נחלת ישראל עמוד תמד הערה נא. [420] ארחות שבת פי"ט סעיף רפו, שש"כ פ"כ הערה רמו. [421] ארחות שבת פי"ט הערה תנ. [422] כנ"ל. [423] ע"פ הנ"ל. [424] שש"כ פ"כ סעיף סח, עב.

פרק יג - טלטול בשינוי

[425] סימן שיא סעיף ח. [426] פשוט. [427] מ"ב סימן שח ס"ק קטו, שעה"צ סימן שלז סק"ז. [428] מ"ב שם, וע"ע חזו"א סימן מז ס"ק יד שיש לו שיטה אחרת בדין טלטול מן הצד ולדעתו רק דוגמא הראשונה מותרת, ועיין ארחות שבת פי"ט סעיף רמו והערה שם. [429] שעה"צ סימן שלז סק"ז. [430] סימן שיא סעיף ח, רמ"א סימן שח סעיף ג ומ"ב ס"ק יט. [431] שם, מ"ב סק"ל, סימן שלח סעיף ז וסימן שי סעיף ו. [432] סימן תקיג סעיף ד, מ"ב ס"ק יב, מ"ב סימן שי ס"ק כב. [433] שעה"צ סימן שלז סק"ז, שלמי יהונתן סימן שיא סק"ו אות ד, וע"ע חזו"א סימן מז ס"ק כא שביאר הדין באופן אחר. [434] סימן שט סעיף א, מ"ב סק"ג. [435] ארחות שבת פי"ט סעיף

[437] שם, רנח ובהערה שעא. [436] שו"ע שם, מ"ב סק"ב, ד. [437] שם, בה"ל ד"ה וי"א, ארחות שבת פי"ט סעיף רנט. [438] סימן שיא סעיף ח, מ"ב סק"ל, תשובת הגרמ"פ בספר טלטולי שבת אות לב. [439] פשוט. [440] שו"ע ומ"ב שם, וע"ע תשובת הגרמ"פ בספר טלטולי שבת אות לב. [441] מ"ב סימן שח ס"ק יג. [442] שש"כ פכ"ב הערה פז ופכ"ח הערה נב, ארחות שבת פי"ט סעיף רנד. [443] מ"ב סימן שיא סק"ל, סימן רעו ס"ק לא, הלכות מוקצה עמוד 40 הערה 11, וע"ע שש"כ פכ"ב סעיף לו. [444] רמ"א סימן שח סעיף ג, ועיין הלכות מוקצה עמוד 40 הערה 13 וספר טלטולי שבת עמוד 232 הערה 16. [445] מ"ב סימן שח ס"ק פב, נחלת ישראל עמוד רג. [446] מ"ב סימן שח ס"ק טו, סימן רעט ס"ק יד, שו"ע סימן שז סעיף ה. [447] רמ"א סימן שיא סעיף ב ומ"ב ס"ק יד, סימן שז ס"ק כב, סח.

פרק יד - מיגו דאיתקצאי

[448] סימן שי סעיף ג, מ"ב ס"ק טז. [449] סימן שי סעיף ז, רמ"א סימן שט סעיף ד. [450] מ"ב סימן שט ס"ק יט, סימן שיח סק"ח, סימן שי ס"ק יט. [451] מ"ב סימן שט ס"ק יט, שבות יצחק ח"א עמוד קפב בשם הגרשז"א והגרי"ש, וע"ע תשובת הגרמ"פ בספר טלטולי שבת אות לג ותהל"ד סימן שי סק"ג. [453] פרמ"ג א"א סו"ס רעט. [454] מ"ב סימן שיח סק"ח. [455] סימן תרלח סעיף ב, מ"ב ס"ק יג, ארחות שבת פי"ט סעיף שע. [456] א"ר סימן שח ס"ק יד, תשובת הגרמ"פ בספר טלטולי שבת אות לה, שלחן שלמה סימן שח אות כו, לוח המוקצה ערך ווקי טוקי/שבור (בחלק המשחקים). [457] מ"ב סימן שח סס"ק לה. [458] רש"י ביצה כד/ב ד"ה אם, ועיין הקדמת המ"ב לסימן תקטו. [459] ארחות שבת פי"ט סימן שעב, שש"כ פ"א הערה קלג. [460] מ"ב סימן שי ס"ק יט. [461] סימן שי סעיף ב, טלטולי שבת עמוד 245, ועיין חזו"א סימן מא ס"ק טז שאינה מוקצה אפילו כשעדיין אינו ראוי. [462] רמ"א סימן שא סעיף מו, מ"ב סימן שח ס"ק סג. [463] מנח"ש סימן י אות ב, מנח"י ח"א סימן פא, תשובת הגרמ"פ בספר טלטולי שבת אות לו, וע"ע שבות יצחק ח"א עמוד קא בשם הגרי"ש"א ואז נדברו ח"א סימן ה דבכל אופן הם מוקצה דלא מהני גמרו בידי אדם במוקצה מחמת איסור, וע"ע קונטרס בעניני מוקצה להגרחפ"ש בסוף ספר שלמי יהודה סימן לא שמחלק בין תלויין בחוץ ובין הכניס למכונת ייבוש. [464] טלטולי שבת עמוד 250, ארחות שבת פי"ט סעיף שפה, מנחת שלמה קמא סימן י אות ז. [465] מ"ב סימן שלו סק"ג, נחלת ישראל עמוד שנ.

פרק טו - ביטול כלי מהיכנו

[466] סימן רסה סעיף ג, מ"ב סק"ו. [467] שם, ספר טלטולי שבת עמוד 212, ארחות שבת פי"ט סעיף שכב. [468] שש"כ פי"ג סעיף

לט. [469] בה"ל סימן רסה סעיף ג ד"ה מפני, ארחות שבת פי"ט סעיף שכה. [470] שו"ע סימן רסה סעיף ג. [471] סימן רסה מ"ב סק"ו. [472] תהל"ד סימן רסו סעיף ז. [473] זכור ושמור מוקצה עמוד 36, שבות יצחק ח"א עמוד ריז בשם הגרש"א. [474] סימן רסה מ"ב סק"ה, שבות יצחק ח"א עמוד רלג, ארחות שבת פי"ט סעיף שכז. [475] סימן רסה מ"ב סק"ה, ארחות שבת פי"ט סעיף שיט. [476] ארחות שבת פי"ט הערה תעב, הלכות מוקצה עמוד 51-52. [477] סימן רסה מ"ב סק"ה. [478] שם, הלכות מוקצה עמוד 52, נחלת ישראל עמוד שצג. [479] שבות יצחק ח"א עמוד רלג, הלכות מוקצה עמוד 52. [480] נחלת ישראל עמוד שצח, ועיין שש"כ פכ"ב סעיף כט, שבות יצחק עמוד רלט-רמא, ארחות שבת פי"ט הערה תפד. [481] שם. [482] נחלת ישראל עמוד שפא, ארחות שבת פי"ט סעיף שכו. [483] שש"כ פכ"ב הערה מה.

פרק טז - מקרים מיוחדים

[484] סימן שח סעיף יח, לד, מ"ב סימן שח ס"ק יג, חזו"א סימן מז ס"ק טו. [485] סימן שח סעיף ו וברמ"א, סעיף יח בה"ל ד"ה הקוץ, מ"ב סימן תקיח ס"ק כא ובה"ל ד"ה אלא. [486] טלטולי שבת עמוד 259. [487] בה"ל סימן שח סעיף יח. [488] שש"כ פכ"ה הערה מו בשם הגרש"ז, חיי"א כלל סז סימן יז, וע"ע חוט שני ח"ג עמוד קח ד"ה והזיקא. [489] חוט שני ח"ג עמוד קח אות ג. [490] סימן שח סעיף לד, מ"ב ס"ק קטו. [491] תהל"ד סעיף מ, גר"ז סעיף עב, חוט שני עמוד קלז, וע"ע ערוה"ש סעיף ס ותשובת הגרמ"פ בספר טלטולי שבת אות לט, ועיין ארחות שבת פי"ט הערה תצ. [492] טלטולי שבת עמוד 267-268, ארחות שבת פי"ט סעיף שלה. [493] עיין טלטולי שבת עמוד 268 הערה *. [494] תשובת הגרמ"פ שם אות לח. [495] נחלת ישראל עמוד תקמא, חוט שני ח"ג עמוד קלח ד"ה אדם. [496] תשובת הגרמ"פ הנ"ל, תשובת הגרש"ז שם אות טז. [497] סימן שח סעיף ד בה"ל ד"ה כלי, וע"ע שבה"ל ח"א סימן קכז אות ד - לא ברור מה רוצים מזה. [498] מ"ב סימן שח ס"ק קלא, קלג, וע"ע חוט שני ח"ג עמוד קלח ד"ה ולכן. [499] עיין סימן שח סעיף לז שמותר רק במקום הפסד. [500] מ"ב ס"ק קלא. [501] חוט שני ח"ג עמוד קלח ד"ה אם, וע"ע נחלת ישראל עמוד תקנג. [502] הלכות מוקצה עמוד 46, נחלת ישראל עמוד תקנ. [503] מ"ב סימן שח ס"ק יג, חזו"א סימן מט סק"ח, פסקי הגרי"ש או"ח עמוד קלג אות לב. [504] מ"ב שם, בה"ל סימן רסו סעיף יב ד"ה יכול. [505] עיין מ"ב סימן תקו ס"ק כט, שש"כ פי"א הערה סט, ארחות שבת פי"ט סעיף ריב, ועיין שש"כ פ"כ סעיף כו. [506] לענין צפרניים וצואת האף עיין שש"כ פי"ד סעיף סב, סט. לענין קשקשים עיין נחלת ישראל סוף עמוד תרצו. לענין שערה ונוצה מבגדו עיין רמ"א סימן שב סעיף א ומנח"י ח"ה סימן לח אות

ג. לענין לכלוך על מאכל עיין ארחות שבת פי"ט סעיף רג. לענין לכלוך על כלי וכסא עיי"ש סעיף רו. לענין זיעה על חלון עיין נחלת ישראל עמוד תרדחצ.   [507] מ"ב סימן שלו ס"ק כד, ועיין שונה הלכות סימן שח סק"י שנשאר בצע"ק בזה, ועיין שבות יצחק ח"א עמוד קח.   [508] מ"ב סימן שא ס"ק קסב ושעה"צ ס"ק רג וסימן שיב סק"ו, ארחות שבת פי"א סעיף כב.

פרק יז - יום טוב

[510] סימן תריא סעיף ב, ועיי"ש בבה"ל ד"ה לקנב.   [511] שו"ת רב פעלים ח"א סימן ל, ששכ"כ פכ"א סעיף ח, מבקשי תורה עמוד תנד (לו) בשם הגריש"א והגרח"ק.   [512] ששכ"כ פכ"א סעיף ד, רמ"א סימן תקט סעיף ז, סימן תקיט סעיף ב.   [513] עיין מ"ב סימן תצט ס"ק כא, בה"ל סימן תקיח סעיף ג ד"ה לקח, ולענין מנורה ותנור חשמל עיין חוט שני יו"ט סוף עמוד צג.   [514] ששכ"כ פכ"א סעיף ד.   [515] ששכ"כ פכ"א סעיף ד, ועיין מ"ב סימן תקטז סק"א.   [516] ששכ"כ פכ"א הערה יז בשם הגרשז"א, הלכות המועדים פ"ז סעיף א, ורע"ע חוט שני יו"ט עמוד צג אות ג.   [517] ארחות שבת פי"ט סעיף שער, ולכאורה א"צ לטעם דיום שעבר דבלא"ה לא אמרינן מגו דאיתקצאי כיון שלא דחיי" בידיים.   [518] עיין מקורות שם.   [519] סימן תקו סעיף ג.   [520] רמ"א סו"ס תקט, מ"ב ס"ק לא, סימן תקיח ס"ק כג, הגהות רע"א למשניות ביצה פ"א מ"ח.   [521] בה"ל סימן תרלח סעיף ב ד"ה וביו"ט, נחלת ישראל עמוד תרנט, מ"ב סימן תקיח ס"ק כד.   [522] מ"ב סימן תקצו סק"ג, רמ"א סימן תרנב סעיף א, סימן תרנד.   [523] סימן תקיט סעיף ב ומ"ב סק"ט.   [524] הלכות המועדים פי"ג הערה 4, נחלת ישראל עמוד תרנט, מ"ב סימן תקיט סק"ט.   [526] רמב"ם הלכות יו"ט פ"א הי"ז.   [527] ד"מ סימן תקמד סעיף ב, מ"ב סימן תרלח ס"ק יד.

May the learning of
this ספר be לעילוי נשמת
and a זכות for the נשמות
of our dear parents

ר' יצחק ב"ר גדליה ז"ל
מרת אסתר בת ר' פישל הכהן ע"ה
ר' אליעזר ב"ר ראובן הלוי ז"ל
מרת שפרה רבקה בת ר' מאיר יוסף
ע"ה

Dedicated by
Judith and Ira Weiss

ת.נ.צ.ב.ה.

Dedicated by

Jonathan Straight

Leeds, UK

In Memory of
His Dear Parents

We would like to express our
deep appreciation to

Harav Yaakov Montrose, shlita,

who has become an inseparable part
of the Guidelines team.

He has demonstrated wonderful expertise
in meticulously checking and editing
the manuscripts of the last seven sefarim.

His experience in the field of halacha
has helped us enormously to ensure
that the rulings in our sefarim
are accurate and conform
to the widespread custom.

May Hashem grant him much siyata dishmaya
in all of his undertakings
and may he merit to continue in the
dissemination of Torah with good health
and menuchas hanefesh.

Rabbi Elozor Barclay   Rabbi Yitzchok Jaeger

Rabbi Yaakov Montrose is the Rosh Kollel of
Kollel Beis Hillel, which is an American
Community Kollel in Ramat Beit Shemesh
with over twenty Avreichim,
and four shiurim daily for balei batim
(for more information, see www.kollelbeishillel.com).
He is also the author of the Halachic World series,
and has over one hundred shiurim
available for free download at
www.halachicworld.com

לע"נ

ר' יוסף שמואל ב"ר אלעזר ז"ל

מרת חנה רחל בת ר' יצחק אריה הכהן ע"ה

Dedicated in Memory
Of our Beloved Parents

Samuel Joseph and Anne Rachela
Barclay

ת.נ.צ.ב.ה.

לע"נ

ר' ישראל ב"ר מאיר טרעפ ז"ל
ואשתו מרת פיגא העניא
בת ר' עובדי' הלוי ע"ה

ת.נ.צ.ב.ה.

Dedicated
to the eternal memory of

הר״ר אלישע מאיר
ב״ר אלכסנדר זושא ז״ל

נלב״ע ח״י אדר א׳ תשע״ו

תנצב״ה

May the learning of this ספר be a זכות
for our beloved parents

ר׳ שלמה ב״ר יעקב יוסף הלוי ז״ל
מרת חיה בת ר׳ פסח ע״ה
ר׳ שמואל שניאור ב״ר יצחק יעקב ז״ל
מרת מרים בת ר׳ שרגא ע״ה

Along with our sister

מרת חיה חנה בת ר׳ שמואל שניאור ע״ה

Dedicated by the Sherwood family

ת.נ.צ.ב.ה.

May the learning of this ספר be a זכות
לעילוי נשמות and be
For our beloved parents

ר' שלמה ב"ר זכריה ז"ל
מרת מינה בת ר' דוד ברוך ע"ה

Henry and Chaya Bauer
Cecil and Lilian Wolpe

ת.נ.צ.ב.ה.

May the learning of this ספר be a זכות and be
לעילוי נשמות
For our beloved parents

ר' זאב ב"ר משה נח ז"ל
מרת גליקה בת ר' שלמה זלמן ע"ה
ר' שרגא פייוול ב"ר מנחם מנדל ז"ל

ת.נ.צ.ב.ה.

ולזכות מרת ברײנדל צביה בת ר' אריה לייב תחי'
לאריכות ימים ושנים

Dedicated by the Vanning and the Berkman Families

לע"נ

אבי מורי
ר' יחיאל מיכל בן ר' בנימין ז"ל

אמי מורתי
מרת רחל בת ר' חיים משה ראובן ע"ה

ת.נ.צ.ב.ה.

With gratitude for all you gave to us

As Hilchos Shabbos and especially
the laws of Muktzeh set us aside
from the nations around us and their ways,
may the learning from this sefer
be a zechus for all those precious neshamos
who have strayed from the path
and bring them back to their
Torah home once again.

לע"נ

ר' ישראל חיים ב"ר שלמה יצחק ז"ל

ת.נ.צ.ב.ה.

לע"נ

ר' אברהם ב"ר שמואל הכהן ז"ל

Dedicated by the Toubin, Dove,
and Kruger families

ת.נ.צ.ב.ה.

לע"נ

ר' שלמה דוד ב"ר ישראל טרעפ ז"ל

נפטר ט"ז כסלו תשע"ח

תנצב"ה

לע"נ

ר' זאב עקיבא ב"ר שמואל ז"ל
ואשתו מרת טויבא בת ר' מאיר לייב ע"ה

למשפחת אהרון

חינכו והעמידו תלמידים הרבה
במשך שנים רבות במלבורן אוסטרלי"ה

ת.נ.צ.ב.ה.

לע"נ

מרת צפורה בת ר' שלום הכהן
ר' יהודה ב"ר יוסף הכהן

ת.נ.צ.ב.ה.

לימוד ספר היקר הזה
יעמוד לזכות ולעילוי נשמת

ר׳ נפתלי יוסף ב״ר שמואל יהודה ז״ל
KRAMER

נפטר א׳ טבת תשע״ו

ת.נ.צ.ב.ה.

Golus with its harsh circumstances
deprived our parents of the
opportunity to learn a lot of Torah.
May our learning of this sefer help
their neshomas to have an aliyah.

Avraham Yaacov ben Moshe Aharon z"l
Hindle Chaya bas Yosef a"h

Pinchas ben Yaacov z"l
Musya bas Aleksander a"h

זכות הלימוד בספר זה תהיה
לרפואתו השלימה
והחלמתו המהירה של

הגאון רבי רפאל משה
בן גיטל (קרלבך) שליט״א
בתושח״י

ונזכה כולנו יחד במהרה לאורו.